Sophie Ravenstone

MASTERING FINANCIAL FREEDOM

Transform Your Mindset to Achieve
Success and Create Wealth

Copyright © 2024 Sophie Ravenstone
All rights reserved.

to Tom,
who taught me how to make more

CONTENTS

Introduction
7

1. Changing Your Thought Patterns
9

2. Establishing Daily Routines
19

3. Developing a Clear Plan
29

4. Networking for Success
39

5. Developing Resilience
48

6. Making Smart Investments
57

7. Diversifying Income Sources
68

8. Gaining Financial Knowledge
77

9. Managing Your Budget
91

10. Achieving Financial Independence
101

Afterword
111

INTRODUCTION

Picture a future in which obtaining financial success and stability is effortless, perfectly aligned with your goals – a future in which your thinking and behaviors automatically attract fortune. Mastering Financial Freedom is designed to help you better understand your money and provide helpful tips for achieving financial independence.

This book is meant to help you develop a way of thinking that brings and keeps success in your life. By using tested ideas and practical steps, you will build a strong base for lasting financial security.

You will begin by looking at how you think, changing any negative beliefs, and creating good habits that help you succeed with money. This book teaches you critical techniques to increase and keep your money, such as savvy investing, good budgeting, and having several income streams.

It is also critical to expand your network, capitalize on your contacts, and persevere in the face of financial difficulties.

By studying and applying this information, you will get the skills and confidence to manage your money effectively and achieve the financial freedom you desire.

Chapter 1. Changing Your Thought Patterns: Shaping Attitudes for Financial Success

Starting the path to financial freedom begins with one important thing: your attitude. How you view money and success greatly affects your financial situation. A magnetic mindset means more than just being positive. It's about changing how you think and feel so you can attract good chances and success. This chapter investigates how to improve your financial condition using effective thinking tactics. Think of your thinking as a powerful magnet that attracts money and success. Just as a magnet attracts metal, your thoughts and beliefs can either attract or repel money and success.

If you understand how your thoughts affect your money, you may use that knowledge to attain your financial objectives. This chapter will demonstrate how a good mindset may transform obstacles into opportunities and lead to long-term success.

You'll start by examining how your present thoughts and beliefs influence your financial status. It's important to identify and deal with any negative thoughts about money so you can achieve your financial goals. As you go through this chapter, you will find useful tips to match your thoughts with your money goals. You will learn how to change negative thoughts into positive statements and use daily mindfulness techniques. This will help you develop a mindset that attracts financial success. By the end of this chapter, you will have the tools and knowledge to build a mindset that helps you achieve financial freedom. Accept these ideas and get ready to think in a way that matches your successful future.

The Power of Thought: How Mindset Shapes Financial Reality

What we think and believe has a big impact on our financial situation. The idea that "thoughts become things" isn't just a saying to inspire people; it's a basic principle that is important for both mental well-being and financial success. How you view and think about money affects how well you can reach your financial goals and build your wealth.

Think about successful business owners who often say that their journey started with one simple idea: they believed they could succeed. For example, Steve Jobs. His goal for Apple went beyond simply developing a computer company; it also included making the world a better place. Jobs was confident in his ideas and ability to succeed. His way of thinking played an important role in his money and job success.

On the other hand, having negative beliefs about money can seriously hold back financial success. For example, if someone thinks that only rich people can have money or that they can never be financially safe, these beliefs can affect how they act and make choices. This kind of thinking can result in missed opportunities, a reluctance to save or invest money, and a failure to progress toward financial goals. If you believe you cannot make money, your choices and actions will usually reflect this perception, making it a reality.

Understanding how your thoughts work means noticing how what you think affects what happens in your life. Instead of saying, "I can't save enough money," you can think, "I am trying to be financially secure." Thinking a little differently can help you create a budget, invest, and find ways to earn more money.

Using pictures in our minds is a great way to help us think better. When you imagine reaching your money goals, like buying a house, starting a business, or enjoying a good retirement, you make a plan in your mind. This plan helps you take steps to reach those goals. Visualization helps you believe in your ability to attain financial success and motivates you to take the necessary efforts.

Furthermore, the concept of a "growth mindset," popularized by psychologist Carol Dweck, holds that we may increase our talents and intelligence by putting up effort and working hard. When it comes to money, thinking about learning and growing can help you deal with money problems and make your financial situation better over time.

In short, how we think can greatly affect our financial situation. What you think about money, how you see yourself, and how you deal with money problems can greatly affect how well you manage your finances. By thinking positively and believing in growth, you can change your financial situation, find new chances, and reach your goals more easily.

Limiting Beliefs: Identifying and Overcoming Mental Barriers

Limiting beliefs are strong notions that might prevent us from earning money and progressing as individuals. These ideas are generally based on prior experiences, what society teaches us, or cultural influences, and they can make it difficult to achieve financial independence. Figuring out and getting past these mental blocks is important for reaching your full financial potential.

Many people believe that only a few lucky individuals can achieve financial success. Many people think that getting rich is something that only those born into money or who have special skills can achieve. This belief can come from what society says or from personal experiences where money felt out of reach. When you think this way, you might unintentionally skip chances, shy away from money risks, or not try to grow. The basic idea is that no matter how hard you try, making money is very difficult.

Fear of failure is a common reason why individuals give up. This perception is generally the result of previous financial difficulties or a lack of confidence in one's own talents. For example, if you have previously experienced financial difficulties or made poor investment decisions, you may begin to believe that you are incapable of handling money. This fear can keep you from doing important things, like putting your money in investments, starting a business, or making good decisions about your money.

To recognize and overcome these mental barriers, begin by reflecting on your past money experiences and how you feel about them now. Examine your views about wealth and success. Do you have negative thoughts that are holding you back? Do you frequently think, "I'm not good with money," or "I'll never be able to save enough"? These thoughts may be preventing you from moving forward.

When you spot these negative thoughts, question them using facts and different viewpoints. For example, if you think you can't earn good money, look for stories of people who had the same problems and were able to succeed. Find stories about people who made money by working hard, learning new skills, and creating good plans. This proof can help you challenge your negative thoughts and encourage a more positive way of thinking.

Change your negative thoughts into positive statements. Instead of saying, "I can't be financially successful," try saying, "I can learn and improve to be financially successful." Changing how you think can help you let go of negative beliefs and create new chances to reach your money goals.

Also, look for help from mentors, money experts, or support groups to guide you and overcome your limiting beliefs. Talking to people who are good with money can give you useful advice and encouragement, which can help you feel even more positive.

To overcome your self-doubts, you need to pay more attention to your thoughts and change the way you think. By seeing and questioning these mental blocks, you can change how you think and build a stronger foundation for achieving financial success. By following this process, you can improve your money skills and grow as a person, making it easier to handle money problems.

Abundance Mentality: Shifting from Scarcity to Wealth

Thinking positively about having plenty can help you meet your financial objectives. A scarcity mentality is the belief that there are inadequate resources and that everyone competes for the few that do exist. An abundant attitude, on the other hand, holds that everyone has various possibilities and resources at their disposal. Changing your way of thinking may vastly improve your financial status and attitude on life.

Fear and competition are common causes of a scarcity mindset. If you believe there isn't enough money, you may continue to look at how much money others have and feel envious or inadequate. Thinking like this can lead to people acting out of fear. They may accumulate too much stuff, pass on fresh investment opportunities, or avoid opportunities to grow out of fear of losing. This creates a loop in which opportunities are lost and money does not increase.

On the other hand, an abundance mindset encourages hope and being open to new ideas. When you think this way, you begin to notice chances instead of problems. For example, if you see financial success as something that is plentiful and possible, you're more likely to take smart risks, look for new chances, and work on improving yourself in your career and personal life. This way of thinking promotes working together instead of competing because you believe there is enough success and good fortune for everyone.

To think positively about having enough money and success, first challenge your views about them. Instead of thinking, "There's only a little bit of money available," consider, "There are endless opportunities for growth and success." Changing your attitude in this way may enable you to address financial issues more constructively and proactively.

Also, I value the opportunity to contribute to the development of a positive mindset. Instead of focusing on what you need, think about what you have. This helps you identify the good parts of your financial condition. Recognizing your accomplishments, no matter how modest, may help you feel fulfilled and delighted.

Keeping a thankfulness notebook, in which you write down what you're grateful for, might help you maintain a happy attitude and feel better about money. Continue to study and improve so that you can be satisfied with your resources. Learning new things and developing abilities increases your value. It demonstrates that you may always improve and evolve. Making connections with people who have a positive outlook and feel there is plenty for everyone can help you grow. Being around people who like working together and want everyone to succeed can motivate you and help you stay positive.

Changing from thinking there is not enough money to believing there is plenty means changing how you think and feel about money and success. By believing that there are many chances out there, being thankful, working on yourself, and building relationships, you can develop a way of thinking that brings in money and helps you do well financially. This change helps you do better with money and also makes your life happier and more satisfying.

Reframing Negative Financial Thoughts into Positive Affirmations

Changing negative thoughts about money into positive statements can really help you think better and do better with your finances. By regularly using positive statements, you can develop a better and more hopeful way to handle your money.

Spot negative money thoughts. The first step to changing negative thoughts is to notice them. Notice the negative thoughts or beliefs you often have about money. You might think, "I will never save enough for retirement" or "I'm not good with money." Write down your negative money thoughts whenever they come up during the day.

Change negative thoughts into positive statements. After you find your negative thoughts, try to change them into positive statements. Instead of saying, "I'm not good with money," you can say, "I am getting better at handling my money every day." Instead of saying, "I can't save enough," say, "I'm working towards having plenty of money, and I'm getting better every day." Make sure your affirmations are clear, written in the present, and focus on the positive.

Incorporate affirmations into your daily routine. Begin your day by repeating your affirmations aloud or silently as part of your regular routine. You can also write them down and post them somewhere visible, such as your mirror, computer, or refrigerator. Regular repetition of these affirmations encourages a positive mindset and keeps you focused on your financial goals. Affirmations might help you cope with financial stress or uncertainty. For example, if you are confronted with a difficult financial decision or a setback, pause and repeat your affirmations to shift your mental state from uncertainty to confidence. This plan can help you see money problems more positively and make better choices.

Track your progress. Look at how positive thinking affects your money habits and attitude. Watch for changes in how you feel about money, your financial choices, and your overall confidence. Think about how these positive statements affect what you do and what happens as a result. Are you noticing that you're taking more control of your money or feeling more positive about your financial future?

Building Daily Mindfulness Practices to Align Thoughts with Financial Goals

Daily mindfulness practices may help you better align your thinking and financial goals. Mindfulness refers to being completely present and aware of one's thoughts, feelings, and surroundings without judgment. When it comes to money management, mindfulness can help you gain a better knowledge of your spending habits, make more informed decisions, and stay focused on your long-term objectives.

Begin with careful awareness of your financial habits. This requires paying close attention to how you manage your money, such as spending, saving and investing. For example, when making a purchase, examine whether it aligns with your financial objectives and ideals. Ask yourself questions like, "Is this purchase necessary?" and "How does this expense fit into my budget and savings plan?" This understanding enables you to make better informed financial decisions and identify areas where you may need to modify your habits.

Develop a mindful budgeting routine. Incorporate mindfulness into your budgeting process by developing a habit that promotes careful financial planning. Set aside time each week to review your budget, track your expenses, and evaluate your progress toward your objectives. During these sessions, practice mindfulness by focusing entirely on your financial evaluation, free from distractions. For example, use this time to reflect on your spending habits, examine your savings techniques, and make any necessary budget adjustments.

Make sure your purchases are in line with your financial goals. Before making a purchase, think about how it fits into your entire financial plan. Ask yourself questions like, "Will this purchase provide long-term value?" and "How will this affect my financial goals?" This will help you avoid impulse purchases and make better financial decisions.

Apply mindfulness techniques to manage financial stress. Financial stress can cause impulsive behavior and emotional expenditure. Deep breathing, meditation, and visualization are all excellent techniques for relaxing and reducing anxiety. Take a few minutes to practice mindful breathing, which involves focusing on your breath while releasing stress.

Incorporating gratitude and introspection into your daily mindfulness practice may assist you maintain a positive financial outlook. Take time every day to reflect on what you are grateful for in your financial situation. Recognize your progress toward your financial goals, the regularity of your income, or the potential to invest in the future. Maintaining a thankfulness journal that focuses on your financial accomplishments and positive experiences may help you feel more abundant and fulfilled.

By incorporating these mindfulness activities into your daily routine, you can enhance the alignment of your thoughts and aspirations. This attentive strategy enhances your financial decision-making abilities, reduces stress, and keeps you focused on your long-term financial objectives. Using mindfulness as a financial management method not only improves your financial situation, but it also leads to a more balanced and fulfilling life.

Exercise: Mindset Journaling: Tracking and Transforming Financial Beliefs

Mindset journaling helps you track and change your financial views. Reflect on your ideas, discover limiting beliefs, and modify them to help you achieve your financial objectives.

1. Make a quiet location and schedule regular journaling sessions to ensure consistency in your practice.

2. Reflect on beliefs. Write down your current financial beliefs and sentiments. Be truthful about your financial thinking.
3. Identify limiting beliefs. Identify reoccurring negative thoughts regarding money. Highlight any beliefs that may be holding you back.
4. Reframe ideas. Replace negative ideas with positive affirmations. For example, replace "I am bad with money" with "I am increasing my financial skills."
5. Visualize success. Describe your ideal financial scenario as if it were already realized. Visualize the emotions and results you want.
6. Make a list of actionable steps for achieving your financial goals. For example, establish a savings goal or develop a budget plan.
7. Review regularly. Return to your journal to keep track of changes and progress. Consider how your beliefs and actions have changed.
8. Seek feedback. Share your insights with a mentor or advisor. Discuss your reflections and receive advice on how to improve your thinking.

What fresh insights have come from this journaling exercise?
How have your reframed views influenced your financial decisions?
What more steps can you take to line with your financial objectives?

Chapter 2. Establishing Daily Routines: Building a Strong Financial Foundation

The foundation of financial success and wealth retention often lies in establishing solid daily routines. Big money plans and investment ideas are important, but it's your everyday habits and routines that really determine your financial future. Daily routines are not just plans for your day; they are strong systems that can affect your financial situation. By using certain money habits every day, you set up a routine that helps you reach your goals and builds good money practices.

We will look at how habits are made, especially how doing something many times can change our behavior for a long time. We'll also look at how rewards might promote excellent financial practices. establishing up a regular program that focuses on understanding your money, checking in frequently, and establishing objectives can help you develop a solid foundation for managing your finances.

This chapter will walk you through simple steps to develop a daily money plan that meets your requirements and goals. By sticking to these habits, you will improve your money skills and develop a strong method for handling your finances. Remember that reaching financial success comes from regularly following these habits. Every little action and daily routine helps you reach your bigger goal of being financially secure and growing your money. Use a daily routine to help you create a better financial future.

The Role of Routine in Achieving Financial Success

Establishing a routine is crucial to financial success. It helps us organize our daily actions and decisions. Financial success does not come from making major decisions or investing enormous quantities of money on a regular basis. It is actually built on regular and consistent practices.

Understanding how our daily habits affect our finances can help us manage and expand our wealth over time.

First, routines give a clear approach and consistency, both of which are required for good money management. When you include money-related tasks into your daily routine, they become regular and less likely to be forgotten. For example, having a set plan for tracking expenses and reviewing budgets ensures that these duties are accomplished on a regular basis. This consistent approach makes money management a natural part of daily living rather than an infrequent effort. Furthermore, doing things on a regular basis helps to reinforce positive money habits via repetition. The study of habits demonstrates that performing the same actions repeatedly causes us to do them automatically after a while. For example, if you make it a practice to save or invest a portion of your earnings every time you receive a paycheck, it will soon feel normal. Over time, these habits really help people build wealth and have financial security.

Another important feature of routines is their capacity to reduce decision fatigue. When making financial decisions on the go, from budgeting to investing, it is easy to become overwhelmed. By incorporating financial decisions into your everyday routine, you may simplify the decision-making process and reduce stress. Setting out a specific day each week for financial assessments, for example, might remove the need for everyday financial decisions, freeing you up to focus on strategic planning rather than urgent problems.

Furthermore, routines encourage accountability and tracking. Regular financial evaluations and check-ins allow you to track your progress and make any required changes. For example, developing a routine for reviewing investment performance or assessing expenditure trends gives insights into your financial health and enables you to make better informed decisions.

Finally, routines encourage long-term success by fostering discipline and control. Financial success typically demands long-term effort and endurance, both of which are enhanced by consistent behaviors. Following a well-structured financial routine helps you develop discipline, which is essential for sustaining financial stability and attaining long-term goals.

In conclusion, routines are essential for financial success because they give structure, reinforce beneficial habits, reduce decision fatigue, promote accountability, and cultivate discipline. Understanding and adopting smart financial routines can help you lay a solid basis for long-term financial success.

Habit Formation: The Science of Repetition and Reward

Habit formation is an important part of achieving financial success, and understanding the science behind it can greatly improve your approach to money management. The process of habit formation is profoundly based in behavioral psychology and neuroscience, and it is critical to our ability to reach and maintain financial goals.

At its root, habit formation is determined by the interaction of repetition and reward. When we continuously perform a given behavior, our brain creates neural pathways that eventually make the behavior automatic. This technique is critical for creating financial habits that will lead to long-term success. For example, setting aside a portion of your income on a regular basis for savings or investments becomes a habit that requires less conscious effort as it gets established in your behavior.

The science of habit development begins with the habit loop, a three-step process that includes trigger, routine, and reward. The trigger initiates the action, the routine represents the behavior, and the reward reinforces the behavior by delivering positive feedback. For financial habits, the trigger could be a specific time of day or event that stimulates you to examine your budget; the routine could be the process of evaluating and adjusting; and the reward could be the joy of staying on track with your financial objectives.

Understanding the loop is critical for developing positive financial habits. To form a new habit, begin by identifying a clear signal and a precise routine that is consistent with your financial goals. If you want to grow your savings, pick a signal, such as the beginning of each month, and make a habit of depositing a predetermined amount of money into a savings account. The reward might be the peace of mind and financial security that a dedicated savings plan offers.

Positive reinforcement also promotes habit development. Rewards for following a financial plan, no matter how little, may greatly increase motivation and adherence. Rewarding yourself with a tiny indulgence or celebrating your achievements can reinforce positive behavior and make it more likely to persist.

Consistency is essential for developing habits. Over time, financial routines lead to the formation of automatic habits that support your financial objectives. The goal is to start small, be consistent, and progressively change your behaviors. As these habits become established, they will assist to provide a firm financial foundation and support your journey to financial success.

How Consistency Compounds into Wealth Over Time

Consistency is an important factor in wealth creation, and its potency stems from how it evolves over time. Consistency in financial management refers to adhering to disciplined procedures and practices that can help you achieve your long-term financial goals. Understanding how consistency works and how it affects wealth growth may provide you a strategic advantage in your financial journey.

Consider compounding, a widely used financial concept. Compounding is the process of generating profits on an investment over time. Whether you invest in a savings account or a retirement fund, your earnings are reinvested and you continue to earn interest on them. This effect increases the growth of your investment over time. Similarly, consistency in financial habits increases your wealth by progressively accumulating favorable outcomes from repeated acts.

Regular savings and investment are one of the most potent methods to impact wealth. You may benefit from the compounding effect by consistently setting away a portion of your paycheck and investing it wisely. Compounded returns enable even little, consistent contributions to savings or investing accounts to grow significantly over time. For example, depositing $100 per month in an investment account with an average annual return of 7% may grow to more than $20,000 in ten years thanks to compounding.

Consistency is also important when it comes to budgeting and cost management. By continuously tracking your expenses and sticking to a budget, you can uncover areas for savings and avoid wasteful spending. This disciplined method aids in the development of an emergency reserve, the reduction of debt, and the release of resources for investment purposes. For example, examining your budget every month and modifying your spending patterns can result in significant savings and increased financial security.

In addition to saving and budgeting, consistent financial education and decision-making help to build long-term wealth. Regularly educating yourself about financial topics, such as investing techniques, tax planning, and market trends, allows you to make informed decisions and react to changing financial conditions.

To summarize, consistency is a powerful driver of wealth accumulation, comparable to the compounding effect of investment. By consistently saving, investing, budgeting, and educating yourself, you can leverage the compounding power of your actions to build and preserve wealth over time. Consistent financial decisions will lay the groundwork for long-term success and financial stability.

Creating a Morning Routine Focused on Financial Clarity

A well-planned morning routine may help you get financial clarity while also setting the tone for a productive day. Developing a morning routine focused on financial clarity means setting certain practices that are in line with your financial goals and will keep you on track. Here's how to develop and implement a morning routine that improves financial well-being.

Begin with a financial evaluation. Start the day by assessing your financial condition. This might include monitoring your bank accounts, reviewing recent transactions, and tracking any investment developments. A brief, 5 to 10-minute assessment each morning keeps you informed about your financial condition and alerts you to any significant changes or patterns. This habit allows you to detect differences early and maintain control over your cash.

Set financial goals for today. Every morning, spend a few minutes outlining specific financial goals for the day. These objectives may include making a payment, reviewing a budget category, or considering a new investment. Setting clear, achievable goals enables you to create a targeted daily plan that aligns with your overall financial objectives. This method ensures that you handle your finances proactively rather than reactively.

Engage in financial affirmations. Incorporate financial affirmations into your morning routine to cultivate a good attitude towards money. Affirmations are positive words that help you redirect your thoughts and achieve your financial goals. For example, you could state, "I am confident in my financial decisions," or "I am capable of accumulating wealth and attaining financial success." Repeating these affirmations on a daily basis will help you change your thinking and gain confidence in handling your finances.

Review your budget and spending plan. Spend a few minutes each morning going over your budget and spending plan. This technique keeps you aware of your financial limitations and guarantees that you stick to your budget throughout the day. By evaluating your budget on a regular basis, you stress the value of financial discipline and make necessary modifications to keep on target. This habit also allows you to anticipate and plan for any upcoming expenses.

Plan for future financial activities. Set aside time to plan any future financial activity or decisions. This could include making appointments with a financial counselor, budgeting for future significant costs, or allocating time to study investment prospects. By proactively planning these chores, you ensure that you are ready for future financial decisions and can make informed decisions that align with your long-term goals.

Incorporate a mindful practice into your morning routine to increase attention and reduce financial stress. Deep breathing and meditation are two mindfulness practices that might help you start the day with a clear and peaceful mind. This activity not only boosts your general well-being, but it also enables you to make more deliberate and prudent financial decisions.

Setting Up Weekly Financial Check-Ins

Establishing a weekly financial check-in is essential for staying in charge of your finances and on track to meet your financial goals. This allows you to analyze your financial situation, evaluate your progress, and make changes as needed. Here's how to efficiently plan and carry out your weekly financial check-ins:

Schedule a regular time. Choose a specified day and time for your weekly financial check-in. Consistency is crucial, so choose a time that works well for your schedule and is free of distractions. Whether it is Sunday evening or Monday morning, setting aside time each week ensures that you prioritize and incorporate this crucial chore into your habit.

Review your budget and spending. Start your check-in by examining your budget and recent expenses. Compare your actual expenditure to your projected spending to identify any discrepancies. Determine if you are sticking to your budget or whether revisions are necessary. This examination helps you understand your spending patterns and pinpoints areas where you may need to cut back or reallocate funds.

Evaluate your financial goals and progress. Evaluate your progress toward your financial objectives. This might include both short-term goals, such as saving for a vacation, and long-term ones, such as establishing an emergency fund. Determine if you are on track to fulfill these objectives and if any modifications are required. Regularly reviewing your goals keeps you motivated and ensures that you are making real progress.

Check investment performance. If you have investments, take time each week to evaluate their performance. Check the status of your investment accounts and see if they are matching your expectations. Look for any obvious changes or patterns that may necessitate your involvement. Understanding your investment performance allows you to make more informed decisions about buying, selling, or changing your investing plan.

Prepare for the projected expenditures. Consider and plan for any future expenses. This includes monthly bills, anticipated payments, and projected purchases. You may avoid shocks by planning ahead of time and ensuring that you have enough money set up. Making a budget for these expenses allows you to control your cash flow and reduce financial stress.

Adjust your financial approach. Based on your research, make any required changes to your financial strategy. This might entail adjusting your budget, reallocating cash, or shifting your investing plan. Regular adjustments guarantee that your financial plan is current and adaptable to changes in your life or financial situation.

Document the key insights and actions. Keep track of the major takeaways and activities from your weekly check-in. Documenting these observations allows you to track your development over time and serve as a reference for future check-ins. Keeping a financial journal can be an effective tool for reflecting on your financial journey and making sound decisions.

Setting up and keeping to weekly financial check-ins can help you build a disciplined approach to managing your resources. This practice improves your financial awareness, keeps you on track with your goals, and enables you to make proactive changes. Incorporating these check-ins into your daily routine will contribute to your overall financial success and stability.

Exercise: Design Your Ideal Daily Financial Routine

Developing a regular financial regimen may significantly improve your money management and help you accomplish your objectives. Follow these steps to create a routine that meets your needs and easily integrates into your everyday life.

1. Clarify your short- and long-term goals. Write them down and prioritize them according to your current requirements and future goals.
2. List your daily financial tasks, such as checking balances, revising your budget, and planning for future costs. This guarantees that you address all essential issues.

3. Set aside specific time intervals every day for financial responsibilities. For example, set aside 10 minutes in the morning for budget review and 15 minutes in the evening for expense tracking.
4. Create a schedule that includes time and tasks. For example, evaluate the balance in the morning, transactions in the middle of the day, and expenses in the evening.
5. Begin adhering to your timetable and monitor its impact. Adjust according to how much time is required and the efficacy of your routine.
6. Keep track of how consistently you follow the routine. Use a journal or an app to record your struggles and triumphs.
7. Evaluate the routine's effectiveness in achieving your financial goals on a regular basis. Make modifications to improve alignment and effectiveness.

Does your routine help you achieve your financial goals? What changes can you make to improve the routine? How has this regimen impacted your overall financial management?

Chapter 3. Developing a Clear Plan: Crafting a Strategy to Draw in Opportunities

A well-planned financial strategy is essential for finding and capitalizing on opportunities. Without a well-planned approach, financial goals might look abstract and out of reach. This chapter stresses the need of developing a specific financial plan in order to capitalize on opportunities and achieve long-term success.

Financial planning is more than just managing your present resources; it also includes formulating a strategy for future growth. It entails identifying your financial goals, developing realistic tactics to accomplish them, and adapting your approach as circumstances change. A comprehensive plan serves as a guide, keeping you focused on your goals and making it easier to capitalize on chances that correspond with your financial objectives.

This chapter will teach you why financial planning is so important for attracting money and how creating SMART (Specific, Measurable, Achievable, Relevant, Time-bound) goals may provide clarity and guidance. You will learn how to modify your approach to the ever-changing financial landscape, keeping your strategy relevant and effective. You will also learn practical ways for breaking down long-term goals into digestible chunks, making your financial path easier to navigate. By the end of this chapter, you will have a thorough understanding of how to develop a strong financial plan and the instruments required to attract chances. This strategic approach will enable you to make more educated decisions, stay focused, and eventually meet your financial goals.

Why Financial Planning is Key to Attracting Wealth

Financial planning is vital for increasing wealth and maximizing opportunities. Without a strategic plan, financial goals may remain hazy and unachievable, but a well-thought-out strategy provides structure and direction, transforming ambitions into achievable goals. You can appreciate the importance of financial planning in earning and conserving money once you understand why it is so vital. So why is financial planning vital?

1. Provides clarification and direction.

A detailed financial plan explains your goals and intended path of action. It helps you define your financial goals, such as retirement savings, home ownership, or starting a business. A financial plan, for example, would describe how much you should save and invest each month in order to retire comfortably. This clarity ensures that your work is targeted and aligned with your long-term objectives.

2. Assists with identifying and seizing opportunities.

With a financial strategy in place, you may better discover and pursue opportunities that match your objectives. For example, if you have a clear plan for saving and investing, you may be better positioned to capitalize on financial opportunities when they emerge. A solid plan enables you to detect these alternatives and make informed decisions rather than reacting impulsively.

3. Ensures effective resource allocation.

You can utilize your resources more effectively if you have a financial strategy in place. You can prioritize your investments and expenditures when you know what your financial objectives are and how to get there. If, let's say, paying off debt is one of your goals, you can set aside a portion of your income for this purpose, which will keep you on track to become financially independent.

4. Encourages long-term wealth building.

A well-developed financial plan encourages long-term wealth growth by creating specific goals and tracking progress. It enables you to make strategic decisions about investments, savings, and spending. For example, reviewing your financial plan on a monthly basis can help you change your approach in response to changing market conditions or personal circumstances, ensuring that you stay on track to meet your financial objectives.

5. Relieves financial stress.

A financial plan lowers uncertainty and stress by outlining a clear way forward. It permits you to predict prospective issues and devise solutions to them. For example, including an emergency fund in your plan can help you ease financial stress amid unforeseen events such as job loss or medical issues.

In summary, financial planning is essential for attracting wealth since it provides clarity, assists in capitalizing on opportunities, allows for smart resource allocation, promotes long-term wealth creation, and decreases financial stress. By building a thorough financial plan, you lay the foundations for meeting your financial objectives and establishing a solid platform for future growth.

Setting SMART Financial Goals for Long-Term Success

Setting SMART financial goals is critical for long-term success because it creates a clear, actionable framework for reaching your financial goals. SMART goals are specific, measurable, achievable, relevant, and time-bound. By following this framework, you may set clear goals that will guide your financial planning and decision-making processes.

1. Specific

Specific objectives are clear and detailed, indicating exactly what you want to accomplish. Instead of broad targets like "I want to save more money," a particular goal may be "I want to save $10,000 for a down payment on a house." This precision enables you to direct your efforts and resources toward a certain objective. For example, if you wish to save for a vacation, provide the place, price, and date.

This clarity offers direction and purpose, making it easier to devise a plan for reaching the objective.

2. Measurable

Measurable objectives establish criteria for monitoring progress and determining if the goal has been met. This usually entails creating numerical targets or benchmarks. For example, if you want to pay off debt, a quantitative objective may be "I will reduce my credit card balance by $500 per month." Having measurable objectives enables you to monitor your progress and make necessary changes. Pace your savings or investment development with financial tools or apps to ensure you stay on track to reach your objectives.

3. Achievable

Achievable goals are realistic and attainable given your current circumstances and resources. This includes determining if the objective is attainable given your income, costs, and other financial commitments. For example, if you earn $50,000 per year, trying to save $100,000 in six months may be unrealistic. Instead, create a challenging but achievable goal, such as saving $5,000 over the following six months. Reachable goals motivate you to work hard while minimizing the chance of failure.

4. Relevant

Relevant goals reflect your entire financial ideals and ambitions. They should be large and contribute to the achievement of your long-term financial goals. For example, if your long-term aim is to retire early, you may opt to raise your retirement savings contributions in the short term. Making your objectives relevant keeps you motivated and ensures that your efforts are directed toward what is truly essential to you.

5. Time-bound

Time-bound goals have a set deadline, which fosters a sense of urgency and accountability. This could be a deadline by which you hope to reach your goal or a timeframe during which you intend to fulfill specific milestones. Setting a goal of saving $2,000 for an emergency fund in three months, for example, provides you with a concrete deadline to aim toward. Time-bound goals help you stay focused and disciplined by establishing a deadline for reaching your objectives.

To summarize, setting SMART financial goals is crucial for long-term success because it gives clarity, allows for progress tracking, assures realism, aligns with your overall goals, and fosters urgency. Applying the SMART framework to your financial goals establishes a solid basis for achieving your objectives and ensuring a secure future.

Adapting Your Plan to Changing Financial Landscapes

Financial landscapes are dynamic, impacted by a range of factors such as economic conditions, market movements, and individual situations. Adapting your financial plan to these changes is critical for maintaining momentum and long-term success. Flexibility and responsiveness ensure that your tactics are relevant and effective even when external and internal elements change. Here's how to adjust your strategy to shifting financial conditions:

1. Monitoring economic and market trends.

Economic conditions and market developments have a considerable impact on financial planning. Monitor economic indicators such as inflation, interest rates, and employment on a regular basis. For example, during an economic downturn, you may need to rethink your investment plan to reduce risks. Keeping an eye on market trends allows you to make informed decisions about asset allocation and investing opportunities. To stay up to date, subscribe to financial news, read market assessments, and consult with financial consultants.

2. Reviewing and adjusting financial goals.

Financial objectives should be reviewed on a regular basis and revised to reflect changes in your financial situation or desires. Work changes, marriage, and having a baby are all examples of life events that might influence your financial priorities and capacities. For example, if you receive a significant raise, you may adjust your savings objectives or investing strategy to take advantage of your better financial status. If you have unexpected costs, such as medical bills, you may need to rethink your savings strategy or reallocate resources.

3. Evaluate investment strategies.

The investment plan should be adaptive to shifting market conditions and personal financial objectives. Regularly assess the performance of your investments and compare them to your financial objectives. For example, if the stock market is erratic, diversify your portfolio with more stable assets. Check your risk tolerance and investment horizon to ensure they are consistent with your current financial situation and goals. Rebalancing your portfolio helps you to keep your desired asset allocation while controlling risk.

4. Adapting to life changes.

Life changes, such as income, expenses, or financial responsibilities, necessitate updates to your financial plan. For example, if you start a new firm, you may need to adjust your budget and financial projections to reflect new income sources and expenditures. Similarly, if your costs rise dramatically as a consequence of a big life event, such as purchasing a home or paying for college, you should adjust your savings and investment approach appropriately. Flexibility is crucial for effectively handling these changes.

5. Implementing contingency plans.

Being prepared for unanticipated events helps you deal with money problems when they arise. Create an emergency fund to cover unanticipated costs, such as necessary repairs or a job loss. Consider your insurance options in order to protect yourself from any risks such as health issues or property damage. Make sure your backup plans are still appropriate for your changing financial condition by reviewing and updating them on a regular basis.

In conclusion, adjusting your financial plan to shifting market and economic conditions means monitoring changes in the economy and markets, examining investment strategies, evaluating financial objectives, responding to life events, and establishing backup plans. Your financial goals will assist your long-term success if you remain sensitive and flexible, even in the face of shifting circumstances.

Breaking Down Long-Term Goals into Actionable Steps

Putting long-term financial goals into reality takes a methodical strategy. The aim is to break down larger goals into smaller, more doable tasks that may be accomplished over time. Here's how to successfully divide long-term objectives into actionable steps:

1. Set long-term financial goals.

Start by carefully outlining your long-term financial goals. These could include objectives such as saving for a house, retirement, or a significant investment. For example, if you want to save $100,000 for a down payment on a house, provide the target amount, time frame, and any other details that clarify the goal. This clarity allows you to create a specific plan and track progress.

2. Set milestones.

Divide your long-term goals into steps. Milestones act as progress indicators, making the entire goal seem more achievable. For example, if you want to save $100,000 over five years, set annual goals of $20,000 annually. These milestones provide a road map and enable you to track your progress over time, making the end objective less frightening and more manageable.

3. Create a comprehensive action plan.

Create a clear action plan for each milestone. This includes determining the steps required to meet each milestone, such as budgeting, saving, and investing. For example, if you want to save $20,000 year, you may set away $1,667 every month. Outline the exact activities you need to take, such as setting up automated transfers to a savings account, cutting needless spending, or growing your income through side employment.

4. Set deadlines and review dates.

Set deadlines and review dates for each stage in your action plan. Deadlines help you remain on track and accomplish projects within a given time range. Set a deadline for each monthly savings goal, and plan regular progress assessments.

5. Adjust as needed.

Prepare to adjust your action plan in response to changing circumstances or new information. Life changes, wage variations, or unexpected demands may need a modification in your plan. If your income reduces, you may adjust your savings objectives or extend the time frame for completing your milestones. Flexibility is required to effectively manage long-term goals and maintain development.

Breaking down long-term goals into specific steps creates a clear and manageable path to financial success. This strategy enables you to stay focused, track your work, and make steady progress toward your ultimate goals.

Using Visualization to Stay Committed to Your Plan

Visualization is a great way to stay dedicated and focused on your financial objectives. Here's how you can use visualization to stay focused on your financial plan:

1. Create a vision board.

Begin by creating a vision board depicting your financial goals. Use visuals, phrases, and symbols that are appropriate to your goals. For example, if you wish to buy a new home, add photographs of houses, communities, and financial goals on your board. Place the vision board somewhere prominent so you may see it every day, acting as a constant reminder of your aspirations.

2. Perform daily visualization exercises.

Include frequent visualization exercises in your regimen. Spend a few minutes each day imagining yourself achieving your financial goals. Visualize the process, the steps you followed, and the satisfaction of meeting your objectives. Consider paying your final house payment or earning a significant investment return. This exercise strengthens your emotional connection to your goals and keeps you motivated.

3. Use affirmations to strengthen your vision.

Combining creativity and positive affirmations will help you stay committed. Create affirmations related to your financial objectives, such as "I am on track to save $20,000 this year" or "I am successfully managing my budget and investments." Repeat these affirmations regularly, envisioning your triumph.

4. Set specific visualization goals.

Define clear visualization goals that are in line with your financial strategy. For example, if you want to increase your savings rate, consider how much you want to save each month and how it fits into your overall goal. Set visual targets for several aspects of your strategy, such as fulfilling milestones, completing tasks, and overcoming obstacles. Specific visualization objectives increase clarity and concentration, improving your ability to stay committed.

5. Monitor your progress and adjust visualization.

Keep track of your progress and change your visualization as appropriate. As you reach milestones or make modifications to your strategy, update your vision board and visualization exercises accordingly. For example, if you hit a large savings milestone, consider the next stage in your path or update your vision board with new goals. Tracking progress and tweaking visualization ensures that your focus remains on your developing goals.

Visualization improves dedication, drive, and clarity in your financial planning. Visualization helps you stay focused on your goals, encourages positive behavior, and promotes overall achievement.

Exercise: Create a 6-Month Financial Action Plan

A 6-month financial action plan entails establishing specific goals, detailing practical measures, and evaluating progress toward your financial targets.

1. Determine specific financial goals for the next 6 months, such as saving a certain amount or reducing debt.
2. Divide your 6-month goals into monthly milestones and indicate the amount of tasks required each month.
3. Create a monthly budget that includes your income, expenses, and savings goals.
4. Plan and organize tasks such as bill payments, money transfers, and investment assessments.
5. Monitor your progress toward your goals and budget, and make adjustments as needed.
6. On a regular basis, go over your plan, evaluate your progress, and make any necessary changes to stay on track.

What are your precise financial goals for the next 6 months, and why do they matter?
How will you track your progress toward accomplishing these goals?
What problems could you experience when putting your strategy into action, and how will you deal with them?

Chapter 4. Networking for Success: Expanding Your Circle to Enhance Wealth

Networking is more than just a buzzword in the business world; it is a vital technique for accumulating riches and creating lasting success. Expanding your circle of contacts can lead to possibilities, resources, and collaborations that you would not have had otherwise. In this chapter, you will learn how strategic networking may greatly improve your financial path, laying the groundwork for accomplishing your objectives and developing success.

The notion of networking extends much beyond simple introductions and business cards. It comprises forming and maintaining relationships to enhance mutual progress and profit. Social capital – the network of relationships you establish and maintain – is essential for your financial growth. These connections may bring valuable information, new investment possibilities, and support during tough times.

Understanding the dynamics of effective networking necessitates a shift in perspective. Instead of perceiving networking as a competitive enterprise, successful people approach it as a collaborative one. By making genuine relationships and concentrating on how you can help others, you may build a network that not only helps you achieve your goals but also improves the lives of others around you.

In this chapter, you will look at the key components of creating a strong network, from identifying the value of social capital to understanding how effective networks offer financial opportunities. You will learn about the change from competition to collaboration and how it may affect your networking strategy.

You will be able to effectively expand your network using practical strategies and specialized insights. By the end of this chapter, you'll have a clear plan for increasing your wealth through smart networking, allowing you to use the power of connections in your financial journey.

The Importance of Social Capital in Building Wealth

Social capital is the value created by the relationships and networks that one builds over time. This intangible asset is sometimes overlooked, but it is essential to financial success and wealth creation. Unlike financial capital, which can be measured in monetary terms, social capital encompasses trust, mutual support, and shared ideals among a group of people. This network may include mentors, peers, industry experts, and even acquaintances who can provide valuable insights and opportunities.

Recognizing the value of social capital is the first step toward developing it. A well-developed network provides access to resources, information, and connections that might otherwise be inaccessible. For example, having a mentor who understands the complexities of financial planning might help you avoid costly mistakes. Similarly, participation in a professional group or industry association may provide access to insider information and job prospects, hastening career advancement and financial security.

Furthermore, social capital can help boost one's credibility and reputation. Connecting with respectable people in your field affects how others perceive you. Increased trustworthiness can lead to opportunities such as high-value projects, investment deals, and commercial partnerships. For example, an entrepreneur with a large network may receive investment offers from reputable investors who believe in the entrepreneur's abilities and the company's potential.

Building and maintaining social capital is more than just making connections; it also necessitates relationship development and trust. Make important relationships, support others, and participate actively in network activities.

Your reputation as a valuable and helpful network member enhances the reciprocal worth of your ties.

In essence, social capital connects you to possibilities that can have a big influence on your financial future. It emphasizes the value of incorporating relationships into your entire wealth-creation plan. By building a strong network and fostering these connections, you create the framework for future success and financial gain.

How Successful Networks Create Financial Opportunities

Successful networks are powerful engines that generate income opportunities. A successful network is defined by its ability to connect individuals with possible collaborators, mentors, and decision-makers who may impact and support their financial objectives. Understanding how successful networks operate can help you harness their power for wealth generation.

The notion of reciprocity is crucial to the operation of every successful network. This principle incorporates mutual benefit, in which both partners in a relationship add value to one other. For example, if you provide your expertise or assistance to someone in your network, they are more likely to respond when you need it. This reciprocal nature generates a dynamic in which opportunities occur spontaneously as a result of mutual aid and common interests.

Furthermore, successful networks promote the exchange of vital information and resources. Connections inside a network might provide exclusive information about industry trends, investment opportunities, and career developments that are not widely known. For example, membership in a professional association may provide you with early access to employment openings or investment opportunities before they become public.

Networking also enhances visibility and access to influential individuals. When you are well-connected, you are more likely to meet key decision-makers who can provide business alliances, finance, or other big chances. Consider how a financial advisor with a large network could be presented to potential investors or clients, broadening their company reach and financial opportunities.

Additionally, effective networks provide a platform for joint initiatives. Strong networks frequently serve as the foundation for collaborative activities such as joint ventures and partnerships. For example, two entrepreneurs with complimentary abilities may work together on a commercial endeavor, using their experience to build a more successful firm than they could alone.

To summarize, excellent networks assist to create financial possibilities by encouraging reciprocity, increasing information flow, increasing visibility, and inspiring collaboration. By actively building and maintaining your network, you position yourself to access and capitalize on possibilities for financial success.

The Mindset Shift from Competition to Collaboration

In the field of networking, there is a significant change from competitive to collaborative. Traditional networking usually emphasizes competition, with individuals contending for limited opportunities and resources. Adopting a collaborative perspective, on the other hand, can help your network grow into a powerful engine for common success and mutual benefit.

Adopting a collaborative mindset means seeing networking not only as a way to promote your own interests, but also as a way to assist others thrive. This change demands recognizing that supporting others in reaching their goals can help you achieve your own. For example, if you connect a colleague with a potential client or offer advice to a peer, you are building goodwill, which might result in mutual benefits. This technique promotes a friendly environment in which interactions are based on trust and mutual aid, rather than competition.

Collaboration requires sharing knowledge and resources. When you approach networking from a collaborative perspective, you are more likely to share useful ideas and opportunities with others. Participating in industry groups or forums, where members share their experiences and resources, can provide you with new approaches, tools, and contacts to help you improve your financial situation.

Another important facet of collaboration is the formation of partnerships. Successful partnerships are usually developed through collaborative interactions in which both parties bring complementary talents or resources. For example, a financial adviser who works with a tax professional may be able to provide more comprehensive services to customers, increasing their client base and reputation. These contacts may result in new business prospects, increased visibility, and mutual success.

Furthermore, collaboration encourages innovation. When diverse perspectives and ideas are combined, they frequently lead to new answers and strategies. A collaborative network increases your chances of discovering unique ideas and strategies that can help you achieve financial success.

Going from a competitive to a collaborative mindset in networking will significantly improve your financial prospects. By stressing mutual support, sharing resources, developing collaborations, and promoting creativity, you can create a network that not only supports your goals but also helps others succeed, benefiting everyone involved.

Identifying Key People to Connect with in Your Field

Developing a solid network begins with finding and communicating with key people who can help you progress financially and professionally. Here's a realistic technique for locating and contacting these key individuals in your field:

1. Determine your objectives. Begin by defining your networking goals. Are you seeking mentors, potential business partners, industry experts, or investors? Your objectives will help you find the proper people.

2. Research industry leaders. Identify notable persons in your sector who are known for their knowledge and influence. Find out who is making waves by reading industry magazines, using internet platforms, and connecting with professionals.

3. Leverage professional networks. Use platforms like LinkedIn to discover and connect with professionals in your industry. Look for people with comparable hobbies or roles that are relevant to your ambitions. LinkedIn's search capabilities and group memberships can help you make new contacts.

4. Attend conferences, seminars, webinars, and networking events relevant to your industry. These events provide opportunity to meet key individuals and form early contacts. Make a list of attendees and speakers who share your networking goals.

5. Seek referrals. Ask coworkers, mentors, or industry contacts for advice on people who would be good additions to your network. Personal referrals frequently result in higher-quality interactions and warm introductions.

6. Determine the potential value of each link by considering how their skills, influence, or resources coincide with your goals. Prioritize those who can provide valuable insights, opportunities, or support.

7. When reaching out, tailor your approach to each individual. Highlight specific reasons why you respect their work or why you believe collaborating would be mutually beneficial. Personalizing your message raises the likelihood of a positive reaction.

By using these steps, you may intentionally develop a network of critical people who will help you achieve your financial and career goals. Identifying and engaging with the proper individuals ensures that your networking efforts are targeted and effective, resulting in important opportunities and progress.

Building Genuine Relationships through Active Listening

Effective networking is based on the development of honest and long-lasting relationships. Active listening is an essential skill for building these connections. Here's how you can utilize active listening to build real relationships and broaden your financial and professional network:

1. Be fully present. When conversing, focus solely on the speaker. Avoid distractions like checking your phone or considering your response while they are speaking. Being present shows respect and indicates that you value what they are saying.

2. Ask open-ended questions. Encourage a more in-depth discourse by asking open-ended questions that attract extensive responses. Instead of asking yes/no questions, learn about their experiences, problems, and ambitions.

3. Reflect and paraphrase. Reflecting on what the speaker has said demonstrates your understanding and engagement. Paraphrasing or summarizing key points simplifies their message and demonstrates active listening. For example, "It looks that you are quite enthusiastic about innovative financial ideas. Could you please tell us how you approach them?"

4. Empathize and validate. Recognize the speaker's emotions and opinions. By empathizing with their emotions or obstacles, you can affirm their experiences. Phrases like "I can see how tough that would be" or "That is a fantastic accomplishment" might help you connect and create trust.

5. Share relevant insights. Once you have thoroughly grasped the speaker's point of view, contribute any pertinent ideas or experiences from your own. This exchange of information should be mutually beneficial and add to the conversation. For example, "I just faced a similar situation, and this is how I handled it."

6. Follow up thoughtfully. After the conversation, provide a specific message or activity that demonstrates your attention and thanks. This may be a thank-you email, an article on their hobbies, or a request for a future meeting. Following up strengthens the connection and demonstrates your care for the relationship.

7. Be authentic. Authenticity is critical in creating authentic encounters. Be yourself, and act authentically. Authentic interactions increase trust and respect, making relationships more meaningful and long-lasting.

Active listening enhances your capacity to build strong, authentic relationships within your network. This strategy fosters deeper relationships, opens up new opportunities, and supports your financial and professional growth.

Exercise: Create a Networking Map and Action Plan

Create a detailed networking map and action plan for efficiently connecting with prominent people in your business. This activity will assist you in organizing your networking goals, identifying essential people, and developing a clear plan for establishing useful relationships.

1. Determine what you hope to achieve through your networking activities. Are you looking for mentorship, business collaborations, or new opportunities? Clearly define your goals.

2. Make a list of people you want to connect with. Include industry leaders, possible mentors, and recognizable experts who share your objectives.
3. Separate your contacts into groups based on their relevance to your goals. Mentors, peers, industry experts, and potential collaborators are among the possible categories.
4. Gather information about every person on your list. Examine their professional history, recent accomplishments, and areas of competence.
5. Determine how you will handle each interaction. Determine the best method of introduction, whether through email, LinkedIn, or in-person events. Tailor your approach to each individual's preferences.
6. Make a plan for reaching out to each contact. Set specified dates for submitting connection requests, scheduling meetings, and following up on early relationships.
7. Make a note of your interactions with each contact using a tracking system, such as a spreadsheet or CRM application. Keep a record of important details, follow-up dates, and notes from your interactions.
8. Regularly examine and adjust your networking map and action plan. Assess your success, make any adjustments, and set new goals to ensure continuing growth and effective networking.

What are your key aims for developing professional network, and how do your contacts contribute to these objectives?
How can you tailor your approach to each interaction in order to make your outreach more successful and engaging?
How will you maintain and deepen connections with your contacts over time?

Chapter 5. Developing Resilience: Overcoming Challenges and Staying on Track

A robust plan and a well-stocked bank account are insufficient to assure financial stability. It is about developing the mental and emotional strength to deal with the unavoidable ups and downs of money management. In this chapter, we will look at how to build resilience so you can overcome financial challenges and stay on pace for success.

Life's financial journey is rarely simple. Setbacks, such as unforeseen costs, economic downturns, or financial losses, are unavoidable during the procedure. Recognizing that these setbacks are unavoidable is the first step in developing resilience. Accepting this fact allows you to face challenges head on, rather than being caught off guard.

Building mental fortitude takes more than simply keeping optimistic; it also necessitates the development of particular skills and strategies for dealing with stress and hardship. Resilience entails staying focused on your financial goals in the face of adversity. It is about learning from failures and using them to achieve future success. This chapter will discuss the nature of financial losses, the importance of mental strength, and how to view failure as a stepping stone rather than a stumbling block.

The practical application of these principles is crucial. You may better prepare for financial crises by setting up a personal emergency fund and developing your problem-solving skills. This chapter will lead you through the practical steps and provide specific recommendations to help you establish a resilient mindset. You will learn how to anticipate potential problems, plan for setbacks, and maintain focus on your financial goals.

Finally, developing resilience entails equipping yourself with the tools and mindset to deal with the unpredictable nature of financial life. With the right measures in place, you can turn obstacles into opportunities while remaining on track for financial success.

Why Financial Setbacks Are Inevitable

Financial setbacks are an unavoidable element of both personal and business finances. These setbacks, which range from unforeseen expenses to market downturns, are not outliers, but rather natural components of the financial environment. Understanding why setbacks are unavoidable is critical for building resilience and ensuring financial stability.

First, life and business are intrinsically uncertain. Economic conditions alter due to changes in government policy, global events, and market dynamics. For example, a rapid economic downturn or a shift in political atmosphere can have an influence on investments, job security, and overall financial health. Even with thorough planning and risk management, external circumstances might cause financial losses.

Second, personal situations often change unexpectedly. Medical issues, job loss, and unexpected home repairs can all put a burden on your finances. These events are frequently beyond one's control, and their consequences can derail even the most well-structured financial plans. For example, someone who has diligently saved for years may face a financial setback if they have a sudden health crisis that requires considerable medical bills.

Furthermore, financial losses might result from inherent risks in investment and commercial activities. Investments in stocks, real estate, or startups may result in losses owing to market volatility, business failure, or economic changes. Entrepreneurs and investors frequently face setbacks when navigating the uncertainties of their companies. Regardless of original strategy and investment, a company may experience financial issues as a result of unforeseen market conditions or operational challenges.

Understanding that setbacks are a natural part of the financial path enables people to approach financial planning with a more resilient perspective. Recognizing the inevitability of these challenges, rather than becoming disheartened by them, aids in good preparation and strategy. This perspective adjustment is critical for establishing the mental fortitude required to overcome hurdles and keep moving forward toward financial goals.

In conclusion, financial failures are unavoidable due to the unpredictable nature of the economy, personal life changes, and the inherent dangers in financial undertakings. Accepting this reality and planning for probable setbacks can help you handle financial obstacles and retain long-term security.

Building Mental Fortitude to Overcome Financial Challenges

Developing mental fortitude is critical for overcoming financial obstacles and keeping on track with your financial objectives. Mental fortitude is the capacity to maintain strength, focus, and determination in the face of hardship. To successfully handle financial issues, you must have a strong attitude that can resist stress, disappointment, and barriers.

Emotional resilience is an important aspect of mental fortitude. This entails controlling stress and remaining cheerful in the face of financial difficulties. For example, when an unexpected expense occurs or an investment underperforms, emotional resilience allows you to remain calm while making sound judgments. Mindfulness, meditation, and stress management strategies can all help you build emotional resilience. By engaging in these techniques on a daily basis, you can better handle the emotional impact of financial issues while remaining focused on your long-term goals.

Another crucial aspect of mental fortitude is the capacity to keep a growth mentality. A growth mindset is the attitude that difficulties and failures provide chances for learning and improvement. Instead of perceiving setbacks as insurmountable challenges, people with a growth mindset see them as opportunities to learn new skills and tactics. For example, if a business effort fails, a person with a growth mindset will examine what went wrong, learn from the event, and apply the lessons to future endeavors. This strategy builds resilience and allows you to adjust to shifting financial situations.

Setting and sticking to specific financial objectives is an essential component of developing mental strength. Well-defined goals provide motivation and direction, allowing you to keep your focus even when faced with obstacles. Break down your long-term goals into smaller, more attainable milestones so you can track your progress and celebrate your victories along the way. This method will help you stay motivated and increase your desire to conquer obstacles.

In addition, seeking advice from mentors, financial advisors, or support networks may help you strengthen your mental power, because these people may offer advice, insight, and assistance in navigating difficult financial situations. Surrounding yourself with a supportive network helps you build resilience and learn how to manage your money wisely.

The Role of Failure in Long-Term Financial Growth

Failure, while frequently seen unfavorably, is essential for long-term financial success. Seeing failure as a learning opportunity, rather than a problem, can yield major emotional and financial benefits. Understanding this perspective is crucial for converting difficulties into opportunities for success.

More significantly, failure teaches us valuable insights about how to develop. Every failure teaches us what went wrong, why it happened, and how to keep it from occurring again. If a company's plan fails, identifying the root causes, such as a lack of market research or poor financial planning, can help design better future plans. This continuous learning helps you to improve your skills, make better judgments, and better comprehend money.

Second, making errors allows you to get stronger and better at adapting. Resilience is the capacity to recover from adversity and achieve one's goals even when conditions are difficult. Handling and getting past failure helps build this skill and gets them ready for future difficulties. For example, an investor who has lost a lot of money might start being more careful and wise about how they invest. This can help them notice market changes and handle risks better.

Furthermore, failure might lead to new ideas and innovations. When first attempts fail to yield the desired outcomes, individuals typically seek other solutions and approaches to the problem. Finding inventive solutions to problems may result in new ideas and possibilities. If a product launch fails, a firm may opt to pivot and develop a new product that better satisfies the demands of its clients, which might lead to greater success.

Failing helps us set realistic goals and deal with risks more effectively. Understanding that making mistakes with money is normal helps people plan better and take fewer risks. People who know that things can go wrong and plan for it can come up with backup plans and make good decisions to reduce future losses.

Failing helps us learn to manage our money better as time goes on. It helps us learn important lessons, makes us tougher, sparks new ideas, and helps us understand dangers better. Viewing failure as a chance to learn instead of a setback can help you reach long-term success.

Creating a Personal Emergency Fund

An emergency fund is an important part of being financially strong. It gives you money to cover surprise costs and tough times. Creating and keeping this fund helps you handle money problems without getting in the way of your long-term goals. Here's a simple guide to help you set up and take care of your emergency savings.

1. Figure out how much you need. Begin by finding out how much money you should have in your emergency fund. A common suggestion is to save enough money to cover your living costs for three to six months. This amount should pay for basic needs like rent, bills, food, and getting around. Adjust the number based on your own situation, taking into account things like how stable your job is and your personal money responsibilities.

2. Open a different savings account just for your emergency money. This account should be easy to access, but not so easy that you want to use it for things that aren't emergencies. Online savings accounts usually have better interest rates, making them a great choice for building your emergency fund over time.

3. Set up automatic savings. Make saving easier by scheduling regular payments to your emergency fund. Decide how much money you can save each month without overspending, and then set up automatic transfers from your main checking account to your emergency fund. Using automation makes it easier to keep adding money to your fund regularly, so you don't have to worry about it.

4. Regularly look at your emergency fund to make sure it's enough as your financial situation changes. For example, if your cost of living goes up or you have more things to take care of, change your savings goals to match. Checking your fund regularly helps you stay ready for any surprise money problems.

5. Make saving for your emergency fund your top goal in your money plan. Consider it a recurring expense, similar to your bills or loan payments. Making this fund a priority demonstrates how important it is in your financial plan and helps it develop gradually over time.

6. Refill the fund after use. If you spend money from your emergency fund, make sure to replenish it as soon as possible.

Setting up and keeping a personal emergency fund is an important first step in being financially strong. By taking these simple steps, you can create a dependable safety net that helps you feel secure and stable when money problems arise unexpectedly.

Developing Problem-Solving Skills to Navigate Financial Hurdles

Good problem-solving skills are essential for dealing with money concerns and maintaining financial stability. To hone these talents, you must actively seek out, comprehend, and resolve financial issues. Here's a useful way for strengthening your problem-solving skills:

1. Identify the core issue: begin by determining exactly what the financial issue is. This entails identifying and distinguishing the underlying cause from the outcomes. For example, if you are having difficulty paying your expenses, it is possible that you need to improve your money management skills rather than simply not earning enough. Knowing the root cause simplifies the problem-solving process.

2. Obtain important information: collect any essential information regarding the incident. This includes financial reports, budgets, and cost lists. For example, if you are suffering with debt, gather information on all of your invoices, such as the amount owed, the interest rate, and the due date. Understanding the complete scenario allows us to make better decisions.

3. Think of possible solutions. Come up with ideas to fix the money problem. Think about different ways to deal with the problem. For example, if you have a lot of credit card debt, some ways to handle it could be talking to your lenders to get lower interest rates, combining your debts into one, or making a clear plan to pay it off. Look at each choice to see if it's doable and how much it could help.

4. Choose the best solution. Look at the advantages and disadvantages of each possible option. Think about things like money, how long it will take, and what will happen in the future. For example, when deciding between combining your debts into one or making a repayment plan, check which choice has better conditions and fits your money goals. Choose the solution that best solves the main problem and fits with your overall money plan.

5. Begin implementing the solution you chose. Make a clear plan that lays out the steps needed to implement the solution. For example, if you want to combine your debts, look into different choices, apply for a loan to help you, and use that money to pay off your existing debts. Following the plan makes sure the solution works properly.

6. Check and change: regularly look over what you found to make sure your solution is working well. Watch how things are going and change plans if needed. For example, if your plan to combine your debts isn't reducing your debt as much as you hoped, think about changing it and making updates if necessary. Paying attention helps you stay focused and adjust to new challenges that come up.

Exercise: Write a Financial Resilience Plan for Potential Setbacks

Improve your problem-solving abilities by approaching a financial situation in systematic phases, resulting in a clear plan and increased resilience.

1. Clearly explain your financial situation and how it impacts you. Explain the problem properly so that we can see how large it is.
2. Gather any essential papers and information about the problem, such as invoices or statements, to assist you in finding a solution.
3. Make a list of at least three possible responses. Consider numerous problem-solving strategies and their possible usefulness.
4. Consider each solution's practicality and consequences. Choose the most effective and simple solution for your issue.
5. Make a list of the actions you'll need to do to implement your solution. Set clear actions and deadlines to follow.
6. Implement the plan. Begin by following the procedures you indicated, and keep track of your progress to confirm that everything is operating properly.
7. Check your plan on a frequent basis to verify it is functioning properly. Change things as needed to get better outcomes based on what you observe.

What problems did you face during this process?
How has the solution affected your financial situation?
What changes would you make to future problem-solving?

Chapter 6. Making Smart Investments: Growing Your Wealth with Strategic Choices

Investing is an important way to build and increase your money, but it can seem overwhelming to a lot of people. This chapter tries to make the process easier to understand, giving you the information and tools you need to make smart investment choices. Smart investing isn't just picking stocks or bonds; it's about knowing the basic ideas that help you make good investment choices and how they can benefit you.

You will start by looking at the relationship between risk and reward, which is an important idea in investing. Understanding that different investments have different risks and possible returns helps you make choices that fit your money goals and comfort with risk. Next, we will explore compound interest, which can greatly increase your earnings over time. When you learn how your money can grow a lot over time, you'll see why it's important to start saving early and keep adding to your investments regularly.

Another important part of smart investing is spreading out your money. This strategy means putting your money in different types of investments to lower risk and increase possible profits. Spreading out your investments can help keep your money safe and improve your chances of making steady profits.

This chapter will help you find investment opportunities that match your money goals using hands-on activities and easy steps. You will learn how to create an investment plan that matches your goals and how much risk you are comfortable with. Whether you're new to investing or want to improve your approach, the tips and ideas shared here will help you create a strong base for lasting financial success.

By the end of this chapter, you will understand the basics of investing and be ready to use a plan that helps your money grow well.

Understanding Risk and Reward in Investing

Investing always means finding a balance between risk and reward. This is a key idea that influences every financial choice in investing. Risk is the chance that what you actually earn from an investment will be different from what you hoped to earn, which can mean you could make money or lose money. On the other hand, reward means the possible benefits or profits an investor could get from their investment.

The risk-reward balance is an important idea in investing. Usually, the chance of making more money comes with a greater risk. For instance, putting money into new companies or growing markets can lead to big growth, but it also has a lot of risks. On the other hand, government bonds usually give lower profits but are safer. Knowing this balance helps investors pick investments that match their comfort with risk and their money goals.

Investment risks are the different ways you can lose money when you invest. Investors face a variety of hazards, including the danger of market fluctuations, the risk of people failing to repay loans, and the risk of being unable to rapidly sell their investments. Market risk refers to fluctuations in asset prices induced by changes in market circumstances. For example, stock prices can go up or down depending on how the economy is doing or how well a company is performing. Credit risk is the chance that a borrower might not pay back money they owe, which can affect investments in bonds or loans. Liquidity risk means having trouble selling an investment quickly without lowering its price. This is important for investors who need cash right away.

Before you start investing, it's important to understand how much risk you can handle. Risk tolerance shows how well you can handle changes in your investment's value without getting worried. Things that affect how much risk you can take include your financial situation, your investment goals, how long you plan to invest, and how comfortable you feel about market ups and downs. For example, younger investors with more time to invest may be willing to take greater risks in order to gain more money. People approaching retirement, on the other hand, may prefer to continue with safer assets in order to protect their funds.

To invest successfully, it is important to identify the right risk-reward ratio for your situation. Diversifying assets across asset types achieves this balance and reduces risk. For example, a diverse investment portfolio could comprise stocks, bonds, and real estate. This helps to offset the impact of one type not performing adequately.

To put these ideas into practice, begin by establishing clear investment objectives and choosing how much risk you are willing to accept. Pick investments that match your goals and how much risk you're okay with. Check your investments often and make changes as needed to keep them balanced and in line with your changing financial situation and goals.

Knowing how risk and reward work together helps you make smart investment decisions, which can lead you to reach your money goals.

The Power of Compound Interest Over Time

Compound interest is an effective investment method that can dramatically increase your money over time. Compound interest, as opposed to simple interest, takes into account both the original sum and any past interest payments. This effect can cause your investments to expand rapidly.

How does compound interest work? Compound interest occurs when the money you earn from interest generates additional interest. So, if you put money in a bank, you will get interest on your savings. Then, the next time interest is computed, it will include the money you earned previously. This means that your money will grow faster over time.

Compound interest means that the money you receive from your assets is reinvested, allowing you to earn even more. If you put $2,000 in an account with a 5% annual interest rate, you will receive $100 in interest the first year. The next year, interest is calculated on the new total of $2,100, resulting in extra interest. This compounding effect accelerates the rate at which your investment grows over time by earning interest on prior interest.

Compound interest exerts a substantial influence over time. The sooner you start investing, the more you will profit from interest accrual over time. For example, investing $5,000 at a 6% annual interest rate for 30 years is much more profitable than investing it for only ten years. This is because there is more time for interest to accumulate and compound.

The Rule of 72 is a simple method for calculating how long it will take for your investment to double assuming a stable yearly return rate. Divide 72 by your yearly interest rate to find out how long it will take to double your money. For example, if you get an 8% yearly return, your money will have nearly doubled within nine years.

Making frequent payments can increase the benefits of compound interest. For example, if you deposit $100 into an account every month at a 7% annual interest rate, you will earn more money over time than if you put in the same amount all at once. This strategy takes use of the benefits of generating interest on your investments over time, as well as the concept of investing a specific amount of money on a regular basis, regardless of how the market performs.

To maximize compound interest, invest early, reinvest returns, and make regular increases. Do not withdraw your money too soon because it will reduce the amount your investment grows over time. Consider assets with high interest rates or returns, and prepare for the long term to take advantage of growth opportunities.

Understanding how compound interest works is crucial for long-term financial growth. If you make sensible decisions and let your money grow over time, you can enhance your wealth and move closer to your financial objectives.

Diversification: Spreading Risk to Increase Return

Diversification is an important investment strategy that helps lower risk and improve potential earnings by spreading money across different types of investments and industries. The idea of diversification is that different investments can do well or poorly in different market situations. Putting your money into different investments helps protect your savings from losing a lot if one investment does poorly.

Diversification means spreading your money into different types of investments like stocks, bonds, real estate, and products. This can also include investing in different industries and countries. This plan aims to lower risk because different assets react differently to changes in the market. For example, when the stock market is not doing well, bonds or real estate might do better, which can help keep overall earnings steady.

Spreading out your assets minimizes the risk of losing money. Having various forms of investments implies that if one item loses value, another may gain value, balancing it out. Diversification helps reduce big price swings and can result in more steady returns over time. For example, a mix of investments in technology, healthcare, and consumer goods might change less in value than putting all your money in just one of those areas.

You have many options to spread out your investments:

1. Asset allocation. Put your money into different types of investments, like stocks, bonds, and cash. Each sort of investment has its own set of risks and potential profits.

2. Sector diversification is investing in a variety of fields, including technology, finance, and energy. This prevents your investment portfolio from becoming overly reliant on one area's performance.

3. Geographic diversification entails investing in markets outside of your own country. This plan is intended to mitigate the risks associated with a particular country's economic challenges.

Adding a range of investments reduces risk, but too many can reduce profits and complicate management. Having too many assets can make it difficult to focus and reduce the chances of achieving a large profit. It is vital to vary things while focusing on a few key areas.

To properly diversify, first examine your current investments and determine whether you have too much money concentrated in one sector. Choose different types of investment options like mutual funds or ETFs, which provide a wide range of choices in different assets. Keep checking and changing your investments regularly to make sure you have a good mix based on how the market is changing.

Diversification is a strong way to reduce investment risk and seek steady profits. By spreading out your investments and regularly checking how they're doing, you can improve your financial security and chances for growth.

Identifying Low-Risk Investment Opportunities

Finding reliable investment options is critical for building a secure financial future, especially for novices or those who wish to limit their risk of losing money. Here's how you can locate these chances.

1. Assess your risk tolerance.

Know what you're comfortable with. Determine how much danger you can bear. This is defined by your financial goals, the time frame you have to achieve them, and the degree of risk you are willing to tolerate.

Check your finances. Before investing in safer choices, be sure you have enough money set aside for emergencies and no high-interest debt.

2. Look for safe ways to invest your money.

Government Bonds: Consider US Treasury bonds, which are government-backed and yield a consistent but low profit.

High Quality Corporate Bonds: Look for bonds from respectable companies with strong credit ratings. These often involve less risk than shares.

3. Check out safe mutual funds and exchange-traded funds.

Bond Funds: Invest your money in mutual funds or ETFs that focus on government bonds or high-quality corporate bonds. They provide diversification while minimizing risk.

Dividend-delivering Stocks: Choose shares from companies that have a history of paying out regular dividends. These can offer greater stability than growth stocks.

4. Consider saving using certificates of deposit.

High-Yield Savings Accounts: Unlike typical savings accounts, these accounts provide greater interest rates, making them a safe method to store money.

Certificates of deposit (CDs) are savings accounts in which you can deposit money for a predetermined period of time. They offer constant interest with low risk. Understand that there is a cost to withdrawing money early.

5. Evaluate Real Estate Investments:

Regarding the Real Estate Investment Trusts (REITs): You can invest in real estate by buying REIT shares. This allows you to benefit from property markets without incurring the risks associated with direct home purchases.

Rental Properties: Purchasing property to rent out can be a profitable investment provided it is well-managed and located in desirable areas.

6. Consult a financial specialist.

To receive personalized suggestions and guarantee that the assets you select are suitable for your risk tolerance and objectives.

7. Important Points to Consider:

Distribute your investments, even if they are secure.

Research and Reviews: Check the performance and stability of your chosen assets on a regular basis to verify they continue to match your low-risk requirements.

By carefully selecting and maintaining safe investment options, you can build a solid financial foundation while generating steady, predictable returns.

Setting Up an Investment Portfolio Aligned with Your Goals

Creating an investing portfolio that corresponds with your financial goals needs strategic planning and careful asset selection. Here's how to create a portfolio that reflects your goals and risk tolerance:

1. Define your financial goals.

Short-term goals: identify goals you want to attain in the next 1-5 years, such as saving for a vacation or a down payment on a home.

Long-term goals: outline targets that are at least ten years away, such as retirement savings or supporting a child's schooling.

2. Determine your risk tolerance:

Assess your comfort level: determine how much risk you are willing to take given your financial status and investing horizon.

Evaluate financial stability: before making investments with varied risk levels, make sure you have a robust emergency fund and a low level of high-interest debt.

3. Select appropriate asset classes.

Equities: invest in stocks that have the potential for growth. Diversify your portfolio by including large-cap, mid-cap, and international equities.

Bonds: use government or high-quality corporate bonds to ensure stability and consistent income. Bonds can offer low risk and predictable returns.

Cash and cash equivalents: keep some money in savings accounts or money market funds for liquidity and security.

4. Allocate assets based on goals and risk tolerance:

Strategic allocation: divide your investments across asset classes based on your objectives and risk tolerance. A more aggressive portfolio, for example, may include a higher amount of shares, whilst a conservative portfolio may concentrate on bonds and cash.

Rebalancing: review your portfolio on a regular basis and alter it to maintain the correct asset allocation. Rebalancing ensures that your portfolio remains in line with your financial objectives and risk tolerance.

5. Consider diversification.

Reduce risk by diversifying within each asset type. For example, when investing in stocks, select firms from various sectors and countries.

Diversify by investment type. Incorporate a variety of investments, including mutual funds, ETFs, and individual stocks or bonds.

6. Monitor and adjust your portfolio.

Regular reviews: review the performance of your portfolio on a regular basis and make modifications as appropriate to reflect changes in your goals, financial circumstances, or market conditions.

Seek professional advice. Consult a financial advisor for specific advice and changes to your portfolio strategy.

Setting up a well-structured investment portfolio that is linked with your goals and risk tolerance will allow you to properly manage your investments and strive toward financial success.

Exercise: Create a Beginner's Investment Strategy

Understanding your goals, risk tolerance, and investing possibilities are all necessary when developing a beginner's investment plan. Follow these steps to create a firm foundation:

1. Define your financial goals.

Short-term goals: make a list of goals that you want to attain within the next 1-5 years, such as saving for a vacation or purchasing a gadget.

Long-term goals: identify goals that are at least ten years away, such as retirement or home ownership.

2. Assess your risk tolerance.

Risk comfort level: determine how much danger you are willing to take. Are you more risk-averse or willing to take on greater risk in exchange for a bigger possible return?

Financial situation: evaluate your financial soundness, including your emergency reserve and outstanding bills.

3. Choose investment types.

Equities: choose a percentage of your portfolio to invest in equities for growth.

Bonds: designate a percentage for bonds to give stability and revenue.

Cash: set aside some funds for cash or cash equivalents to ensure liquidity and safety.

4. Allocate Assets.

To allocate assets, create a balanced portfolio with shares, bonds, and cash based on your risk tolerance and goals. For example, you might invest 60% in stocks, 30% in bonds, and 10% in cash.

Diversify within categories: choose a variety of investments within each asset class, such as different sectors of stocks or different bond kinds.

5. Set up investment accounts.

Brokerage account: create a brokerage account to begin buying and selling investments.

Consider opening a retirement account, such as an IRA, for tax benefits.

6. Regular monitoring and rebalancing.

Track performance: review your investment portfolio on a regular basis to ensure that it is on track to meet your objectives.

Rebalance as needed: make frequent adjustments to your asset allocation to preserve your preferred risk level and investment mix.

What are your top three short- and long-term financial goals, and how will your investment plan help you reach them?
How willing are you to take investment risks, and how does this affect your asset allocation?
What steps will you take to guarantee that your investment plan is constantly reviewed and adjusted as needed?

Chapter 7. Diversifying Income Sources: Increasing Financial Stability

In today's changing economic landscape, putting all of your financial eggs in one basket can be risky. Having multiple means to create money is not just for people who are talented with money; it is critical for financial security and freedom. This chapter addresses why it is critical to have different methods to generate money and how having a variety of income streams may help you maintain your finances.

The concept of having many means to earn money extends beyond simply working a second job. It is necessary to establish a solid financial foundation based on a variety of income sources. This can help to keep the economy steady and growing even while it is struggling. Having multiple means to earn money allows you to avoid relying on a single income and can be beneficial when money is tight.

Let us begin by discussing why having multiple means to earn money is vital for obtaining financial independence. Making money from a variety of sources protects you from financial difficulties and unexpected economic fluctuations. This strategy not only improves your financial status, but it also allows you to achieve your long-term goals faster.

We will then explain the contrast between passive and active income. Active income is acquired through hard work, whereas passive income is earned with minimal effort after the first task is accomplished. Knowing these types will assist you in selecting and managing money sources that are suited for your lifestyle and financial objectives.

Finally, we will discuss how diversifying investments can reduce financial risk. Just as having a variety of investments can help you deal with market changes, having a choice of ways to earn money can save you from losing your job or seeing your business fail. This chapter will give you practical information on how to identify and build different ways to make money, allowing you to have a more secure and profitable financial future.

Why Multiple Income Streams Lead to Greater Financial Freedom

Depending on just one way to make money can be risky, especially since jobs and the economy can be unstable and uncertain. Having different ways to earn money helps build a stronger financial base. It's important to have different ways to make money if you want to be free and stable with your finances.

Having many income streams might help you avoid financial troubles. If one source of income becomes insufficient or is eliminated, other sources of income can still provide the necessary funds. For example, if you lose your primary work, income from renting out property, assets, or a second employment might assist pay for daily expenses and alleviate financial concerns.

Having many ways to make money allows you to accumulate riches faster. Every additional technique to earn money helps you improve financially. It allows you to invest more, save more effectively, and reach your financial objectives faster. Consider a person who works full-time, freelances on the side, and makes money by renting out a house. Having many sources of income allows people to develop their wealth faster than relying just on one salary.

Having many sources of income might also provide you with greater options and financial flexibility. Having many means to generate money provides you the freedom to make financial decisions that align with your objectives and values. For example, earning money without working, such as through investments or royalties, allows you to explore different careers or take a sabbatical without worrying about money.

Knowing the two types of income – active and passive – is essential for diversifying your assets. Active income is money earned by working directly, such as receiving a salary or pay from your employment. On the other hand, passive income is money received with minimal work after the initial setup. This might be from investments, rental properties, or money from artistic efforts. Managing both forms of income may increase your financial security and wealth.

Finally, the key to gaining financial independence is to consistently manage and develop your revenue streams. By having many income sources, you strengthen your financial foundation, increase your chances of wealth growth, and have more control over your financial future.

Passive vs. Active Income: Understanding the Differences

To successfully integrate several methods of earning money, it is necessary to grasp the difference between passive and active revenue. Both are essential for financial stability and growth, but they work in different ways and provide various advantages. Understanding how different forms of income contribute to your financial strategy can make it simpler to establish a robust and secure portfolio.

Active income is money you make by working regularly and putting in effort. This includes money earned from jobs, salaries, commissions, or freelance work. Active income is money earned based on the amount of labor you do. The more hours and work you put in, the more money you will earn. For example, a full-time job pays you consistently based on the number of hours you work or the tasks you complete. Similarly, a consultant gets paid for each project or client with whom they work. Active income is critical for meeting everyday expenses and is frequently the only source of income for many people.

Passive income, on the other hand, is money produced with minimal continuous effort once the initial labor is accomplished. This type of income typically comes from assets or enterprises that generate revenue on their own without requiring a lot of work all the time. Passive income examples are money you earn without working actively. This includes money from renting out property, profits from stocks, payments for books or music you created, and earnings from a business where you don't have to be involved every day. For example, having rental properties can give you regular money with little work needed after you set them up and take care of them at first. In the same way, if you invest in stocks that pay dividends, you earn money from the stocks you own, not from what you do every day.

Understanding the advantages of various kinds of income will enable you to design a strategy that suits your immediate financial demands while also working toward your long-term objectives. Active income provides immediate money and helps you maintain stability, while passive income allows you to accumulate wealth and financial freedom over time. By combining the two, you may produce a range of income streams to help you achieve your financial goals and adapt to changes in your life and the market.

The fundamental goal is to use both types of income to boost your financial security and growth. Active income is what helps you stay financially stable right now, while passive income helps you build wealth over time and become financially independent. Mixing different ways of earning money helps you create a stronger and more adaptable budget, giving you a good foundation for future financial success.

How Diversification Reduces Financial Vulnerability

Diversification is a key approach for reducing financial risks and increasing long-term stability. You may reduce risks and protect yourself from potential financial issues by investing your money in a variety of locations and sorts.

Diversification means spreading your money over a number of investments, income techniques, and financial assets. This method helps reduce the effect of bad results in one part on your overall financial situation. For example, if you have money in stocks, bonds, property, and mutual funds, a drop in one area might be balanced out by steady or rising value in another. This balanced method lowers the chance of big losses and raises the chances of steady gains.

In simple words, diversification means making money from different ways or sources. Depending only on one way to earn money, like a salary from a full-time job, can put you at risk if something happens to that job, like if you lose it or if your pay goes down. Earning extra money through part-time job, rental properties, or investments creates a safety net that helps you to stay afloat even if one of your income streams is interrupted. This technique guarantees that money is received on a consistent basis, eliminating dependency on a single source of revenue.

Also, spreading out your assets might help you deal with economic shifts and market fluctuations. For example, during difficult economic times, certain places may struggle greatly, but others may remain stable or even thrive. If you have a variety of assets, you are less likely to be adversely affected if one performs poorly. This approach helps maintain your finances solid and adaptable to market changes.

Using diverse risk-mitigation strategies involves meticulous preparation and continuous monitoring. It is vital to examine your current financial situation, identify ways to invest in various things, and make sound selections based on your goals and the level of risk you are ready to tolerate. You can enhance and adjust your financial situation by distributing and earning money in a variety of ways. This protects you against unexpected disasters and improves your financial stability over time.

Identifying Potential Side Hustles and Passive Income Sources

1. Evaluate your skills and interests. Start by examining your abilities, hobbies, and interests. Consider those activities you excel at or like. If you are competent in graphic design, you could choose freelancing work or selling digital products.

2. Identify market opportunities. Examine current trends and market demands to uncover prospective side hustles. Look for gaps or niches that match your skills. For example, if there is a growing need for online teaching and you are knowledgeable in a specific field, this may be a lucrative side job.

3. Consider passive income ideas. Once established, passive income streams need little continuous work. Investing in dividend-paying equities, developing an online course, or monetizing a blog or YouTube channel are some possibilities. Investigate various passive income possibilities to find which one best meets your interests and financial goals.

4. Consider investment alternatives. Look at a variety of investment possibilities that can give consistent income. Real estate investments, peer-to-peer lending, and the creation of digital goods like e-books or online courses are all feasible funding sources. Determine the potential profits and hazards for each choice.

5. Evaluate your time and resources. Determine how much time you can commit to a side hustle or passive income project. Check that you have the necessary resources, such as equipment or start-up cash, to get started. For example, starting a blog may entail an investment on a name and hosting service.

6. Make a plan. Create a detailed plan including your chosen side hustles and passive income sources. Establish specific objectives, timelines, and action plans for developing and managing these initiatives. For example, if

you are starting a freelance business, explain how you will recruit clients and manage your workload.

7. Start small and scale up. Test one or two side hustles or passive income sources to verify their viability. Once you have gained experience and seen positive results, consider extending or adding new streams to boost your financial security.

Reinvesting Extra Income to Create More Wealth

1. Track your extra income. Begin by keeping accurate records of any additional income you receive from side hustles, investments, or other sources. Maintain detailed records with a financial tracking program or app. For example, if you earn $500 per month from freelancing work, document it.

2. Establish clear financial goals. Set financial goals for reinvesting additional cash. Decide whether you want to save for retirement, invest in stocks, or launch a new business. Clear goals will direct your investments approach. For example, you may want to invest in a diverse portfolio to increase your wealth over time.

3. Select investment vehicles. Research and choose investment instruments that are compatible with your objectives and risk tolerance. Stocks, mutual funds, real estate, and high-yield savings accounts are all possible options. For example, you may elect to invest additional money in index funds for long-term gain.

4. Automate reinvestments. Set up automatic contributions to your preferred investment accounts to ensure constant reinvestment of excess income. Automation decreases the likelihood of missing contributions and facilitates systematic wealth accumulation. For example, set up monthly transfers from your checking account to your investing account.

5. Monitor and adjust. Review the performance of your investments on a regular basis and make any necessary changes to your approach. Monitor results and reassess your objectives to ensure that your reinvestment strategy remains on track. For example, if your assets are underperforming, consider adjusting your portfolio or looking into other investment opportunities.

6. Reinvest earnings. Use any earnings or dividends from your investments to build your wealth. Reinvesting these revenues can help you prosper over time. For example, if you receive $200 in dividends, reinvest it in extra stock.

7. Conduct an annual review. Perform an annual evaluation of your reinvestment strategy and financial objectives. Make adjustments based on your accomplishments, income fluctuations, or changes in your financial goals. For example, if you earn a large bonus, consider increasing your reinvestment amount.

By systematically reinvesting excess income, you can speed wealth building and improve your financial security.

Exercise: Create a Plan for Adding Two New Income Streams

This activity will assist you in identifying and planning for two new revenue streams to increase your financial security.
1. Identify your interests and skills. Make a list of your skills, hobbies, and interests that could be used to generate cash.
2. Research potential opportunities. Investigate several ways to produce revenue depending on your talents and interests. Look into options such as freelancing, consulting, and producing digital goods. Consider platforms that allow you to provide online classes or seminars.
3. Evaluate market demand. Check market trends and competition to see whether there is a viable audience.

Look at online discussion boards or social media groups related to your job to see what topics others care about.
4. Set clear goals that you can measure for each new way to make money. Decide how much money you want to earn and how long you want to take to do it. For example, create a goal to make an extra $500 per month from freelancing in the following six months.
5. Create a clear plan. Make a list of the procedures involved in developing each method of earning money. List the essential duties, what you'll need, and the important dates.
6. Assign resources. Figure out what you need, like time, money, or tools. Make a plan for how to use these resources to start making new money. Think about setting aside money for marketing costs or buying software.
7. Put plans into action and monitor how they are performing. Change your plans based on how things are going and what others say. For example, if you're not earning as much money from freelancing work as you expected, consider modifying how you sell your services.
8. Review and make changes. After a few months, assess how effectively each new method of producing money is performing. Adjust your objectives and plans based on what you learn.

What talents or interests can you use to generate more income?
How can you verify that your new revenue sources are in line with current market demands?
What problems can you have while utilizing these income sources, and how can you overcome them?

Chapter 8. Gaining Financial Knowledge: Enhancing Your Wealth Through Education

Learning is an important tool for achieving financial independence since it may transform the way you develop money. Financial education is more than just understanding how money works. It is about understanding what you need to know to make sound decisions, comprehend investments, and deal with economic fluctuations. As you begin this section, you will discover how understanding money may help you make better decisions and achieve long-term success.

Many individuals struggle with money because they do not know how to manage it effectively. Financial literacy teaches you about fundamental skills such as budgeting, investing, and debt management. It demonstrates how these factors interact to influence your total financial condition. By understanding more about money, you may avoid common mistakes, make smarter decisions, and secure your financial future.

This chapter looks at how important education is for achieving financial success. We'll explore how learning about money helps you understand chances, evaluate risks, and create good plans. Also, keeping up with the latest money trends and news is important for adjusting to changes in the market and taking advantage of new chances.

You will learn easy ways to improve your money knowledge. This includes finding helpful tools and making a learning plan just for you. If you use the right method, you can turn what you learn about money into practical steps that help you make more money.

In this chapter, you will learn important ideas and also practice skills to use what you've learned. When you keep learning, you can gain more control over your money and achieve success. Get ready to improve your money knowledge and open up new ways to grow and take care of your wealth.

The Importance of Financial Literacy in Wealth Creation

Understanding money is essential for developing and sustaining wealth. It involves the information and abilities needed to make wise and prudent financial decisions. People who do not grasp basic financial principles may struggle to manage their money, invest wisely, and prepare for the future. This section discusses why knowing money is crucial for generating wealth and how it may help people make better financial decisions.

1. Understanding money skills.

Financial literacy means understanding important topics like making a budget, saving money, investing, handling debt, and planning for retirement. It needs an understanding of basic ideas like interest rates, inflation, managing risk, and how to divide investments. People who are good with money can handle complicated financial products, understand what's happening in the market, and make smart choices that match their money goals.

2. Smart budgeting and handling money.

One of the main advantages of understanding money is that you can make and control your budget. A good budget helps people keep track of their money, decide what to spend on, and save for things they want in the future. Knowing how to budget helps people find where they spend too much money, decide what is important to pay for, and change their spending to reach their goals.

For example, someone who knows how to manage money might set aside part of their income for an emergency fund. This can help them feel safe if they have unexpected costs. By learning how to budget, people can stop living from one paycheck to the next and build a strong financial base.

3. Smart choices about where to put money for the best results.

Knowing about money is important for making smart investment decisions. Knowing about different types of investments like stocks, bonds, mutual funds, and real estate helps people create a varied investment portfolio. Knowing ideas like risk and return, how long to invest, and compound interest helps people pick investments that fit their willingness to take risks and their money goals.

For example, someone who knows compound interest can make long-term investments that rise significantly. They may use their knowledge to make wise decisions that will build their wealth and help them achieve financial independence.

4. Good debt management.

Handling debt is an important part of understanding money. People who know a lot about managing debt can look at loan details, interest rates, and how to pay the money back. They can come up with plans to pay off high-interest debts, like credit card bills, without borrowing too much money.

Someone who is adept at managing debt, for example, may opt to pay off high-interest credit cards first and then only pay the lowest amounts on lower-interest loans. This strategy saves interest fees and allows you to pay off debt faster.

5. Preparing for retirement.

Understanding money is very important for planning for retirement. Knowing about retirement accounts like 401(k)s, IRAs, and pensions helps people make smart choices about saving for when they stop working. Knowing things like how much money you can put in, how taxes affect your savings, and what investment choices you have helps people create a retirement plan that keeps them financially safe later in life.

For example, a person might save money often in a retirement account and use extra money their employer adds to it. By realizing how important it is to start saving early and to put in as much money as possible, they can ensure a nice retirement.

6. Understanding money products and services.

Financial literacy helps people understand how to make smart choices about money and financial services. When picking a mortgage, insurance policy, or investment account, it's important to understand the rules and details. This helps people choose the options that are right for them.

For example, a person who knows the difference between fixed-rate and adjustable-rate mortgages can pick the loan that fits their financial situation and future plans.

All in all, understanding money is very important for building wealth. It helps people learn how to handle their money well, make smart choices about investments, manage debt properly, plan for retirement, and understand financial products. By improving money knowledge, people can create a solid financial base, reach their goals for building wealth, and ensure a successful future.

How Education Translates into Smarter Financial Decisions

Education is very important for making smart money choices. It gives people the knowledge and skills they need to handle money matters well.

1. Making choices based on information.

Individuals with more education are better at making financial decisions. When people grasp basic financial principles, they may make better judgments and choose solutions that align with their financial objectives. Understanding the fundamentals of stocks, bonds, and mutual funds, for example, allows customers to choose which investments are best for them depending on their risk tolerance, investment time horizon, and financial goals.

For example, someone who knows about investment strategies might choose to put their money in a mix of low-cost index funds instead of expensive mutual funds. Making a smart choice can help you have better money results in the future by lowering investment costs and increasing profits.

2. Strategic financial planning.

People may learn how to create and manage effective financial plans through education. Understanding basic financial planning principles such as budgeting, saving, and goal setting enables people to design strategies that address their present and future requirements. People may improve their money management and achieve financial independence by setting specific financial objectives and developing plans to achieve them.

For example, someone who appreciates the value of retirement planning may create a 401(k) account and make monthly contributions to it. They would also benefit from their employer's matching contributions and tax benefits. This proactive method supports a successful retirement and alleviates financial difficulties in later life.

3. Managing risk and staying safe.

A thorough financial education entails knowing how to handle risks and the principles of insurance. Knowing about various types of insurance, such as health, life, and property insurance, allows people to protect themselves and their things from unforeseen circumstances. Furthermore, financial education teaches people how to analyze and eliminate risks, allowing them to make informed decisions about their money.

For example, a well-informed individual may opt to get adequate health insurance, preventing them from spending a large sum of money out of pocket. They could look at life insurance options to keep their family financially secure if they die unexpectedly.

4. Avoiding common money mistakes.

Education helps people avoid typical financial difficulties and blunders. Many people struggle with money because they do not comprehend financial goods and services. People who learn about money can avoid costly mistakes and make decisions that will help them achieve long-term financial health.

For example, knowing how much high-interest debt affects you can help people avoid having too much credit card debt. People who have education are more likely to use credit wisely, pay their debts on time, and stay away from high-interest loans that can harm their finances.

5. Understanding money products and services.

Education helps consumers how to understand and choose financial products and services correctly. Understanding the various financial products, such as loans, credit cards, and investment accounts, allows clients to select the best solutions based on their specific needs and financial goals.

For example, a person who understands the laws of different mortgage kinds can choose between a fixed-rate and an adjustable-rate mortgage based on their financial circumstances and future goals. Choosing attentively like this allows them to choose the best goods while avoiding issues.

To sum it all up, learning about money enables you to make better financial decisions. It educates people how to make healthy financial decisions. They can establish effective financial strategies, manage risks, avoid mistakes, and select the appropriate financial products. People who learn about money can improve their financial management skills, make more sound decisions, and attain more financial security and success.

Staying Informed: Keeping Up with Financial Trends

Keeping up with financial trends is critical for making sound decisions and keeping ahead in wealth accumulation. This section discusses why it's vital to remain current on financial trends, how they affect our decisions, and how to stay educated in a rapidly changing financial environment.

1. Adjusting to changes in the market.

Money markets and the economy are always changing. Keeping up with these changes helps people adjust their money plans as needed. For example, changes in interest rates, inflation, and market conditions can greatly affect how much money you earn from investments, how much it costs to borrow money, and how much your savings grow. By understanding these trends, people can change their investments, saving methods, and financial plans to match what's happening in the market today.

For instance, when interest rates go up, people might think about switching their investments from bonds to stocks because higher interest rates can make bond prices drop and stocks might give better returns. Keeping up with these trends helps people change their money plans when needed.

2. Using new money options.

Keeping up with money trends allows people to discover and take advantage of new opportunities to create money. New financial products, more investment opportunities, and regulatory changes can all bring up new avenues for growth. For example, new technology has generated digital assets and cryptocurrencies, which provide fresh opportunities for investors who stay up to date on the newest developments.

Also, changes in government rules and tax laws can affect how people plan their finances and invest their money. Knowing about these changes helps people find ways to save on taxes or change their plans to follow new rules.

3. Improving money skills.

Keeping up with financial changes enhances money knowledge. Knowing what is going on now enables people to make sense of financial concepts and apply them in real life. For example, understanding how rapidly the economy is growing and how many people are unemployed may help us better comprehend the market. This can help clients make better judgments about where to invest their money and how to save.

Also, keeping up with money trends helps you keep learning and improving. It encourages people to take charge of their money and helps them handle changes in their financial situations better.

4. Avoiding money mistakes.

Keeping up with money news helps people stay away from common money problems. For example, understanding housing market trends and interest rates might assist consumers avoid making poor investment decisions or paying too much for property. Knowing the regulations of loans can help people avoid costly mistakes while borrowing and managing their debt.

By staying updated, people can spot and steer clear of possible scams or tricks that might appear when the economy is uncertain. Knowing about current money trends helps people stay aware and keep their money safe.

5. Creating a money network.

Keeping up with money trends means connecting with a group of financial professionals and experts. Joining finance organizations, attending industry events, and participating in online forums may provide you with valuable knowledge and updates on emerging trends. Creating a network of financial advisers, mentors, and peers allows people to see diverse perspectives and stay up to date on new facts.

For example, talking to financial experts can give you helpful advice on market trends, investment plans, and future economic predictions. Being part of a group of people who think like you can help you get support and encouragement to reach your money goals.

In the end, keeping up with money trends is essential for successful financial management and wealth growth. It helps people to respond to market changes, capture new opportunities, improve their financial skills, avoid mistakes, and establish a useful network of financial resources. People who strive to keep current on financial news can make better judgments and finally attain their objectives.

Researching Free Resources to Boost Your Financial Knowledge

In today's digital era, it is easier than ever to receive financial education. The internet provides a plethora of free tools and information to help you learn about money and make financial decisions. Using these tools properly will allow you to learn about money without spending any more funds. Here's how to find and use free tools to improve your financial literacy.

1. Check out online classes and webinars.

Many well-known organizations and colleges provide free online seminars and webinars on financial issues. Coursera, edX, and Khan Academy provide courses on anything from basic money management to complex investing techniques. These platforms usually have courses made by experts, providing a clear way to learn that can help you understand financial ideas better.

Find courses on money management. Begin with classes that teach basic topics like budgeting, saving money, and handling debt. These courses will give you a strong base for learning more about finance.

Consider taking investing or wealth-building classes. After you've mastered the fundamentals, try taking classes in investing, asset management, and retirement planning. These subjects will help you build methods for increasing and protecting your wealth.

Join a live webinar. Many finance experts and organizations hold live online talks about current money trends and ideas. These are a fantastic way to keep informed and communicate with experts.

2. Use financial blogs and websites.

Many financial blogs and websites provide valuable suggestions and information on a variety of money-related issues. Websites such as Investopedia, NerdWallet, and The Motley Fool provide articles, tips, and tools to help you learn about complex financial subjects.

Read personal finance blogs. Search for blogs by money experts and experienced investors. They usually give advice, share their own experiences, and suggest ways you can improve your financial situation.

Read financial articles. Many websites contain information on various money-related issues, such as tax preparation and retirement savings. Reading these articles on a regular basis will help you stay up to date on the latest trends and best practices.

Use helpful tools. Many finance websites offer free tools and calculators to assist you with budgeting, retirement planning, and investment management. These tools can help you use what you've learned for your own financial situation.

3. Check out money-related podcasts.

Podcasts are now a common way to share money tips and lessons. There are many podcasts about money that talk about things like how to invest and tips for managing your money.

Pick podcasts with trustworthy hosts. Find shows run by financial experts or well-known groups. These podcasts probably give good information and helpful tips.

Learn about money topics. Listen to podcasts about different money subjects like investing, saving, and planning your finances. This type will help you understand financial ideas better.

Join podcast groups. Lots of podcasts have online spaces or forums where fans can talk about episodes and share their thoughts. Joining these groups can make your learning better.

4. Join online money groups.

Online forums and social media groups about money can be great places to learn and talk about financial topics. Websites like Reddit's r/personalfinance or Facebook groups about money give you a chance to ask questions, share your experience, and learn from other people.

Take part in discussions about money subjects that you find interesting. Asking questions and talking about what you've been through can help you see things in a new way and find answers.

Ask for help from experts. Many online groups have people who know a lot about money. Try to find chances to learn from people who have a lot of experience and knowledge.

Share what you know. Talking about your ideas can help you understand better and also assist others in the group.

By using these free resources, you can improve your understanding of money and make better choices about your finances. Keep looking for new details and staying informed about money trends. This will help you manage your financial future better.

Making a Learning Plan Focused on Key Financial Topics

Making a defined learning plan is critical for acquiring and applying financial information effectively. A strong strategy allows you to cover everything vital, maintain your drive, and assess how far you've progressed. Here's how to make a concise learning plan that includes key financial topics:

- Determine your financial goals and what you need to learn.

Before learning about money, think about what you want to achieve and what you need to understand the most. This will help you create a learning plan that meets your own needs and goals.

Set your goals. Decide what you want to accomplish with your money. Do you want to get better at budgeting, learn about investing, or get ready for retirement? Knowing what you want to achieve will help you know what to learn.

Check what you know. Look at what you currently understand about money topics. Are there certain things you don't feel confident about? Knowing where you are now will help you pick the best materials and subjects to learn.

Focus on learning topics. Look at your goals and what you already know, then choose the financial topics that are most important for you to learn. This will allow you to focus on the most critical tasks first.

- Choose valuable materials and develop a study plan.

Choose materials that are relevant to what you want to learn and devise a strategy for effectively organizing your study time. This will allow you to stay organized and focused on your study schedule.

Choose good resources. Choose books, online courses, podcasts, and other resources that will help you learn what you want to know. Ensure that the materials are reputable and give actionable suggestions.

Make a study plan. Set aside a specific time each week to study. Maintaining consistency is essential for achieving development. Choose how many hours each week you can honestly devote to studying and stick to your strategy.

Use a variety of learning tools, such as reading, viewing videos, and listening to podcasts, to make your learning more engaging and comprehensive.

- Set specific learning objectives.

Set objectives to monitor your development and keep motivated. Milestones will allow you to keep track of what you've accomplished and guarantee that you're making continuous progress toward your learning objectives.

Create short-term goals. Divide your learning into small, doable tasks. For example, you could set a goal of finishing an online course or reading a certain number of chapters from a book.

Keep track of your triumphs and lessons learned. This might help you understand what you have learned and identify areas for development.

Change your plan as needed. Review your learning plan on a frequent basis and make any necessary modifications. If you discover that some subjects need more time, or if your objectives change, adjust your strategy appropriately.

To increase your financial knowledge, apply what you've learned to your own situation. Try out new methods and ideas to see how they work in real life.

Try new approaches. Use the ideas and methods you've learned to help you with budgeting, saving, investing, and other money-related tasks. This will help you get hands-on experience and see how your learning makes a difference.

Keep an eye on your results. Track what occurs when you make adjustments based on what you've learned. Check to see if the plans are working and make any necessary adjustments.

Consider what you've learnt from time to time and how it has affected your financial situation. Consider strategies to continue studying and expanding your grasp of money.

- Stay involved and keep learning.

Learning about money is an ongoing process. Make learning a regular habit in order to stay on top of money issues and improve your financial management skills.

Always seek for new content, upgrades, and financial trends. Keeping up with things can help you adjust to changes and keep informed about financial issues.

Join financial groups. Participate in financial-related online chats, discussion groups, and social media networks. Talking to and learning from others can help you better understand things.

Set new learning goals. Once you've met your first objectives, create new ones to keep pushing yourself and learning.

You will obtain a strong grasp of money topics if you design and adhere to a study timetable. This step-by-step technique will teach you all you need to know about making sound financial decisions and reaching your financial goals.

Exercise: Commit to a Learning Schedule for One New Financial Skill

This activity will help you create a disciplined plan for learning a new financial skill. Committing to a study plan can help you improve your financial knowledge and remain up to date on current trends.

1. Choose a financial skill that you want to learn, such as budgeting, investing, or understanding tax legislation.
2. Set clear learning goals. Determine what you want to accomplish with this ability. For example, you could wish to create a personal budget or consider several investing options.
3. Choose trustworthy sources like online classes, books, or money-related blogs. Make sure they are current and important.
4. Make a study plan. For example, save 30 minutes every Tuesday and Thursday.
5. Write down important ideas, lessons, and how to use them in real life.
6. Practice the new skill in real-life situations. For example, make a monthly budget using what you know about managing money.
7. Check your progress frequently and adjust your learning plan as needed. Consider what works well and what may be improved.
8. Ask for feedback.

How has gaining this new skill changed your financial decisions or behavior?

What hurdles did you face along your learning journey, and how did you overcome them?

How will you continue to improve this ability to increase your financial understanding and success?

Chapter 9. Managing Your Budget: Maximizing Resources for Long-Term Wealth

A strong budget is critical to financial success. It enables you to manage your money, keep your spending under control, and save for the future. This chapter discusses fundamental aspects of budgeting and provides practical advice to help you manage your money better.

Budgeting isn't just a way to keep track of what you spend; it's a smart way to handle your money so you can reach your financial goals in the future. By learning how to budget well, you can better understand your financial situation, decide what to spend on first, and make sure your money is being used wisely.

We'll start by looking at why making a budget is important for being financially secure and successful. After that, we will talk about different ways to budget, like the popular 50/30/20 rule, and see how these methods can be adjusted to fit your personal financial situation.

This chapter talks about how important it is to make a budget that you can realistically stick to each month. Hands-on exercises will help you develop and track your own monthly budget. This way, you can see how making a budget can improve your financial situation.

By the end of this chapter, you will know how to handle your budget well, use your resources wisely, and build a path for lasting money and financial safety. Let's start this journey to understand money better and use budgeting to reach your financial goals.

Why Budgeting is the Backbone of Financial Success

Budgeting isn't just about money; it's an important habit that helps you reach your financial goals in the long run. Budgeting is really about deciding how to spend your money wisely. It helps you make sure that every dollar you earn is used to support your goals and dreams.

Budgeting is important for several reasons, including obtaining a better grasp of your money. Tracking your income and expenses allows you to see where your money goes and how much you have left to save or invest. This openness enables you to discover areas where you may be overspending and make changes to remain on pace with your financial goals.

Budgeting helps you to prioritize and track your expenditure. A strong budget may help you manage your money wisely for goals such as home ownership, emergency savings, and retirement investment. It also helps you distinguish between what you need and what you want, ensuring that your spending is in line with your long-term financial goals rather than being driven by impulsive desires.

Budgeting can also help you manage your debt better. Sticking to a budget helps you to set aside money on a regular basis to pay off debts, lowering the total amount you owe over time. This technique promotes judicious spending, which helps to minimize current debt while avoiding new debt from being collected.

Making a budget is vital for keeping control of your spending. It demonstrates that you only spend what you can afford, minimize unnecessary expenses, and make prudent financial judgments. This approach is crucial for long-term financial stability and success. It is helpful to ensure that your spending is in line with your financial objectives and beliefs.

The 50/30/20 Rule and Other Effective Budgeting Strategies

Budgeting is more than just keeping track of your expenses; it also entails using solid money management techniques. Among various budgeting systems, the 50/30/20 rule is popular due to its simplicity and effectiveness. This method splits your after-tax income into three categories: what you need, what you desire, and how much you save or pay off debt.

The 50/30/20 rule states that you should spend half of your money on necessities including housing, bills, food, and healthcare. These are the expenses necessary to maintain your current lifestyle. The goal is to spend half of your money on necessities while preserving your savings.

Next, spend 30% of your money on things you want. These are additional expenses such as dining out, having fun, traveling, and purchasing items that are unnecessary. These charges improve your life, but they are not required for you to survive each day. By limiting this category to 30%, you can have fun with your spending while still focusing on your money goals.

You set aside 20% of your money for savings and paying off debts. This part is very important for creating your financial future. It includes putting money into retirement funds, saving for emergencies, and paying off loans. By paying attention to this area, you not only get ready for surprises in your money needs but also aim for lasting financial safety.

Besides the 50/30/20 rule, there are other good budgeting methods that can help with your financial planning. The zero-based budgeting system requires you to allocate every dollar you make to specific expenditures, savings, or debt repayment, so you don't have any leftover money that isn't utilized for something. This strategy helps people manage their money properly, and it is especially useful for those with fluctuating earnings or specified savings goals.

Envelope budgeting is a strategy in which cash is placed in separate envelopes for different sorts of expenditure. This strategy allows you to keep track of how much you spend and establish limitations in various areas, making it ideal for folks who like to handle their finances more directly.

Each budgeting method has its benefits and can be changed to fit your financial situation and goals. No matter if you pick the 50/30/20 rule or another way to budget, the important thing is to find a method that helps you handle your money well and match your spending with your future goals.

How Tracking Expenses Leads to Better Financial Control

Good budgeting requires not just establishing financial goals, but also regularly assessing and monitoring your spending habits. Keeping track of your expenses is an important habit that will allow you to better manage your money and make sound decisions.

Tracking spending includes noting everything you spend, whether it's a monthly charge or an impulse purchase. Keeping track of your spending gives you a good understanding of where your money goes. This practice can help you understand how you spend money and identify areas where you may be overspending or need to make changes.

One of the primary advantages of keeping track of your costs is that it allows you to identify and solve financial difficulties. For example, you may find that little purchases, like daily coffee or subscriptions you don't use much, can add up to a large total over time. Seeing these patterns helps you choose to spend less on things you don't need and use that money for saving or paying off debt instead.

Keeping track of your spending helps make sure you don't go over your budget. It lets you see your spending right away and helps you stay within the limits set for each budget category. Keeping a close eye on your money is very important for staying on track with your budget and financial goals.

Also, keeping track of your spending can help you plan your money better for the future. By looking at past spending records, you can estimate future costs and change your budget if needed. This way, you can get ready for future expenses and handle your money better.

Also, keeping an eye on your spending can make it easier to get ready for taxes and check your finances. Keeping accurate records helps you gather proof for tax deductions, control your money flow, and understand your overall financial situation better.

There are several tools and methods for keeping track of spending, ranging from pen and paper to advanced systems and software. Your preferences and needs will determine which tool is ideal for you. It is critical to keep detailed records of your costs.

Finally, tracking your spending is crucial for effective money management. It shows how individuals spend their money, identifies areas where they overspend, ensures they stay under their budget, and assists them in planning and estimating future expenses. By recording your costs on a regular basis, you may have more control over your money and go closer to achieving your financial objectives.

Creating a Realistic Monthly Budget

Making a practical monthly budget is an important part of managing your money well and building wealth over time. It means looking at how much money you earn and spend so you can manage your money wisely and stay within your budget. Here's how to make a real and practical monthly budget:

1. First, find out how much money you make each month. This includes your paycheck, money you make from side jobs, money from renting out property, interest from savings, dividends from investments, and any other ways you earn money. For people with a salary, use the money you take home after taxes to see how much you really have to spend.

If your income varies, take the average of the last few months to figure out how much you usually earn.

2. Next, create a complete list of all the money you spend each month. Group them into two types: fixed expenses (like rent, bills, and insurance) and variable expenses (like food, fun, and eating out). Fixed expenses stay the same every month, but variable expenses can change. Make sure to include all the important and optional expenses in your list.

3. Sort your spending into different categories to keep better track of your money. Common areas include home, getting around, food, health services, saving money, and fun activities. Make sure each category shows how you really spend your money and what you want to achieve financially.

4. Look at how much money you make each month, then decide how much to spend on each part of your budget. Know what you can really pay for in each area. For example, if you plan to spend $300 on groceries but keep spending $400, either change your budget or try to spend less on groceries.

5. Include saving money and paying off debt in your budget. Save some of your money for emergencies, retirement, and other financial goals. Set aside additional money to pay off debt and improve your finances.

6. After you've created your budget, monitor your spending throughout the month to ensure you stick to the numbers you've set. Budgeting tools, apps, or spreadsheets can help you keep track of your expenditures in real time. If you see any changes or additional expenditure in certain areas, adjust your budget appropriately.

7. At the end of each month, review your budget to evaluate how well it is functioning. Examine any disparities between what you intended to spend and what you really spent. Use this information to better your budget for the coming month. Change your categories and budgets based on your spending habits and financial goals.

By following these steps, you may create a monthly budget that is appropriate for your financial circumstances and aspirations. A healthy budget helps you manage your money properly, prevents you from overspending, and keeps you focused on meeting your long-term financial objectives.

Tracking Spending to Identify Areas for Improvement

Keeping track of your expenses is critical for good financial management and long-term wealth creation. It comprises tracking your spending habits in order to have a better understanding of how you spend your money and identify strategies to save it. Here's how you can track your expenses and use that knowledge to improve your financial situation:

1. Select a method of tracking your expenditure that is appropriate for you and your lifestyle. You can use budgeting software, spreadsheets, or just a pencil and paper. Budgeting software often offer features for automatically tracking and classifying your expenditure. Spreadsheets, on the other hand, allow you to edit and manually enter data. Choose an approach that is simple to implement and sustain.

2. Begin by keeping track of your overall income and expenses. This includes buying items, paying bills, subscriptions, and other expenses. Take notes on the date, amount, and kind of purchase for each transaction. To make things exact, record your expenditure as it happens, or at least once a day, so you don't forget anything.

3. Sort your recorded spending into categories like housing, transportation, food, eating out, fun activities, and saving money. Organizing your expenses helps you see where your money goes and shows you how you spend. Many budgeting apps sort your spending into different groups, but it's important to check and change these groups to match your personal needs.

4. Examine your spending on a regular basis to identify patterns or changes. Look for areas where you frequently overspend or where your spending has escalated. For example, you may realize that you are spending more money than you expected when dining out, or that you constantly overpay for recreational activities. Looking at these trends helps us identify areas for improvement.

5. Examine your spending patterns and identify areas for improvement. For example, if you discover you're spending a lot of money dining out, consider cooking more at home or considering how frequently you want to eat at restaurants. If you spend a lot on groceries, try to save money by planning your meals and keeping a budget.

6. Set limits on how much you can spend in each area according to your budget and money goals. Set practical and reachable limits to avoid spending too much and make sure your costs match your income. Keep an eye on how much you're spending compared to these limits so you can stay on track and make changes if necessary.

7. Use what you've learned from observing how you spend money to make informed budgetary decisions. If you see that certain categories routinely go over budget, consider transferring cash from less vital areas or identifying ways to reduce needless spending. Adjusting your budget based on your real spending helps you manage your money more effectively and improves your overall finances.

8. At the end of each month, review what you spent and consider how you manage your money. Examine your expenditure to determine whether it aligns with your goals and if the improvements you implemented were effective. Consider any problems or victories you've had, and use those lessons to improve your money management and budgeting abilities.

By tracking your spending and understanding your habits, you may figure out where your money is going and make smarter decisions to improve your financial situation. This strategy helps you to assess where you might improve and ensures that your expenditure is consistent with your financial objectives.

Exercise: Build Your Personal Budget and Track it for One Month

This activity allows you to construct a tailored budget and track your costs for one month to obtain insight into your spending patterns and ensure you are on track to meet your financial objectives.

1. Gather all of your income sources and current expenditure documents, such as bank statements, credit card bills, and receipts.
2. Make a list of all the ways you make money, including your job compensation, freelance work, property rent, and any other sources of revenue. Add the amount of money you received each month.
3. Divide your monthly expenses into two categories: fixed expenditures (such as rent, bills, and loan payments) and variable costs (such as food, dining out, and recreational activities). Write down each category and how much it costs.
4. Determine how much money to spend on various activities depending on what you make and how you typically spend. Make careful you spend less than you make.
5. Keep track of your daily expenditures, including how much you spent, when you spent it, and what you spent it on. Use a budgeting app, a spreadsheet, or a notebook to keep track of your money.
6. Look at what you actually spent and compare it to what you planned to spend at the end of each week. Find any areas where you are spending too much or too little money.

7. Change your budget as necessary, based on how you spend your money. If you realize that you are consistently overspending in particular areas, try changing your budgeting or spending habits.
8. At the end of the month, calculate how much you spent. Check to see whether your spending meets your budget and financial goals. Determine whether you need to make any other changes.

How well did your actual expenditure match your budgeted amounts? Were there any categories where you routinely spent more or less?
What changes did you make to your budget during the month? How have these adjustments affected your overall financial health?
What insights did you acquire from tracking your expenses? How will you utilize this knowledge to enhance your budgeting and money management skills in the future?

Chapter 10. Achieving Financial Independence: Steps to Freedom and Control

Financial independence means being good at managing your money. It's when you have enough money from your savings or investments to live how you want, without having to work a regular job. This chapter talks about the key steps and plans you should follow to become financially independent.

Becoming financially independent isn't just about earning a lot of money. It means taking care of your money, trying to grow it, making clear plans, and choosing wisely. It's about shifting focus from just making money to finding a better way that promotes long-term stability and cares for the environment.

In this chapter, you will learn what financial independence means. It's not just a big dream; it's a real goal that needs careful planning and regular effort. You will learn how to create simple goals that will guide you towards financial freedom. We will look at how to go from obtaining items to caring for them so they can grow and stay stable. This move demands a change of perspective and careful planning. It is vital to have a financial strategy to help you achieve your long-term objectives.

You will learn how to calculate the amount of money required to become financially independent, set up automated saves and investments, and develop a clear strategy that fits your financial goals. This chapter will teach you how to manage your money and construct a future in which you may make decisions based on what you care about and want to accomplish.

What Financial Independence Really Means

Financial independence means having enough money coming in from your savings or investments to pay for your living costs. This lets you stop working for a paycheck if you choose to. But to really understand what this means, we need to take a closer look at what it includes and its effects.

Financial independence means having a steady source of money that doesn't rely on a regular job. This can come from different places, like investments, rental homes, or other ways to earn money without active work. Financial independence means being able to live the way you want without always having to work for money.

Identifying your "financial independence number" is a key step toward financial freedom. This is the amount of money you should have saved so that you may earn enough to cover your living expenses indefinitely. To calculate this amount, you must first determine how much money you will spend in the future on housing, healthcare, education, and recreational activities. Then you calculate how much money you need to invest to pay these expenditures using the proceeds from those assets.

Another critical distinction is understanding the difference between being financially independent and retiring early. Being financially independent might allow you to retire earlier, but it is not required. Financial independence entails being able to determine if you want to continue working, pursue your hobbies, or do other things without worrying about money. It enables people to make life decisions based on what they want rather than merely what they need.

To become financially independent, you need to make a plan and manage your money carefully. This means making specific money goals, making a spending plan, and putting money into good investments. You need to keep checking your financial situation and change your plans based on how things change around you and in the market.

Finally, financial independence entails having control over your money and future. It is about living a life in which you can focus on what is actually important to you, like as spending time with family, engaging in hobbies, or donating to causes you care about, without worrying about money.

How to Set Milestones Toward Financial Freedom

Setting financial independence milestones includes breaking down the larger goal of being financially independent into smaller, more doable activities. These key milestones highlight your progress and keep you motivated along the way. You might devise a strategy to achieve financial independence by establishing clear and realistic goals.

The first step in identifying milestones is to explicitly express your main aim. This includes establishing your financial independence number, which is the amount of money you need to survive without working. Once you get this number, you may follow the necessary actions.

- Short-Term Milestones:

These are the first steps that help you reach your big goal. They usually involve things like saving for emergencies, paying off debt with high interest, or beginning to invest in retirement savings. Short-term goals help you build a strong money base and get ready for bigger challenges ahead.

- Medium-Term Goals:

As you move forward, these goals are about growing your money and making your financial situation safer. Examples include saving money for a house, putting money into different types of investments, or reaching certain savings goals. Reaching these goals takes regular work and usually means changing how you budget and spend money.

- Long-Term Goals:

These are important steps that show you are getting closer to your main goal of being financially free. Long-term goals might be getting your investment portfolio to a certain value, earning a specific amount of money without working for it, or reaching a certain level of profit from your investments.

These objectives are often larger and may necessitate several years of careful saving and investing.

Every objective should be SMART (specific, measurable, realistic, relevant, and timely). Instead of setting a broad goal like "save more money," a SMART goal could be "save $10,000 for an emergency fund in the next year." Setting SMART objectives clarifies and simplifies each goal, allowing you to track your progress and adjust your plans as needed.

It is critical to review and adjust your goals on a regular basis to ensure they remain on track. Your life and financial circumstances may change, forcing you to reconsider your goals and revise your plans. You can achieve financial independence by being open to change and responding to it.

To summarize, achieving goals is a key step toward financial freedom. By breaking down your major objective into smaller, more manageable activities, you may create a clear strategy for success and stay motivated along the way.

Shifting from Accumulation to Sustainable Wealth Management

The transition from just getting money to efficiently managing it is a vital step toward long-term financial independence. This transformation requires not just increasing your money, but also ensuring that it continues to provide income and is secure for the future. Sustainable wealth management is the discipline of properly managing your money so that it remains secure and you may live your life as you see appropriate.

Understanding sustainable wealth management: unlike the previous phase, when the primary aim is to build your wealth, sustainable wealth management focuses on conserving and properly employing what you already have. This means using plans to help your money grow while keeping it safe from possible problems. It needs a good mix of growing money and keeping it safe, so you have enough to reach your big goals in the future.

Spreading your investments and minimizing risks are essential components of money management. Investing in a variety of assets, such as stocks, bonds, real estate, and other choices, reduces risk and mitigates the impact of market volatility on your overall investment. Diversification means spreading your money over many assets so that you are not overly reliant on a single one. This helps to keep your wealth safe and secure during tough economic times.

In addition to saving, excellent money management requires you to focus on earning money. This means putting money into things that earn you regular money, like stocks that pay dividends, rental houses, or savings accounts that give you interest. By having different ways to make money, you can live the life you want and reach your money goals without using up your main savings.

Proper estate planning is an important part of long-term financial management. It requires determining how to transfer your assets to your family in a tax-efficient manner while honoring your wishes. Good estate planning safeguards your money for your family's future requirements and can help you avoid future disputes or troubles.

Effective money management necessitates repetition and change over time. As your financial situation, goals, and market conditions change, you should assess your plans and make changes as needed. Looking at your assets, financial plans, and risk management can help you stay on track to achieve your long-term goals.

Identifying Your Target Financial Independence Number

To be financially independent, you must first determine how much money you will need to live your desired lifestyle. Identifying your desired quantity of money for financial independence is a key step in planning for a future in which you have freedom and control over your finances. Here's an easy method for determining your target number:

1. Choose the type of life you desire. Begin by imagining your ideal future life. Consider how much you spend on living costs, trips, hobbies, and anything else that can enhance your life. This will help you figure out how much money you need each year to live the way you want to.

2. Find out how much you spend in a year. Keep track of what you spend now and sort your expenses to figure out how much you will spend in a year. Include all major costs, such as rent, bills, food, transportation, and healthcare. Consider devoting time and money to enjoyable activities such as going to the movies, traveling, and pursuing hobbies. Add up all of these expenses to obtain the total for the year.

3. Remember that prices can go up over time. This is called inflation. When you figure out how much to save, keep this in mind. Plan your yearly budget to handle these future price increases. An expected yearly inflation rate is a normal way to guess how much people will spend in the future.

4. Calculate the average amount of money you expect to make from your assets. This can include earnings from stock, bond, and real estate investments, among other forms of income. The amount of money you make from your investments determines how much you need to save and invest to reach financial independence.

5. Calculate how much money you'll need to live your ideal lifestyle using a safe withdrawal percentage. A simple guideline is to take out 4% of your savings each year. This means you should have 25 times what you spend in a year saved up. For instance, if you spend $50,000 a year, you would need $1.25 million ($50,000 times 25) to be financially independent.

6. Consider your personal situation. Your life, health, and personal goals can affect how much money you need to be financially independent. Consider these factors and adjust

your calculations to ensure that your goal figure is appropriate for your unique scenario.

7. Check in frequently. As your life, spending, and financial circumstances change, monitor your financial independence goal and alter it accordingly to guarantee that your goal remains relevant and achievable.

By following these steps, you may determine how much money you require for financial independence and devise a strategy to achieve that objective. This easy strategy will assist you in establishing clear financial objectives and taking tangible actions toward financial freedom and control.

Automating Savings and Investments to Reach Financial Freedom

Setting up automated saves and investments is an excellent method to achieve financial freedom. You may create automatic procedures to ensure that money is transferred into your savings and investment accounts on a regular basis without having to do it manually. This strategy allows you to stay to your plan, resist the temptation to spend money, and make steady progress toward your financial goals. Here's how to save and invest more easily:

1. First, find out what you want to save for, like an emergency fund, retirement, or a big purchase. Decide how much money you want and when you want to get it. Having a defined aim will allow you to better design your automation.

2. Choose the savings and investment accounts that best suit your needs. Consider high-interest savings or money market accounts while saving. Other avenues to invest include retirement accounts such as 401(k)s or IRAs, as well as conventional brokerage accounts.

3. Schedule regular transfers of funds from your checking account to your savings or investment accounts. Choose how frequently you want to send money (e.g., once a week, every

two weeks, or once a month) and how much you want to send each time.

4. If your employer offers a retirement savings plan, such as a 401(k), be careful to set up automatic contributions from your paycheck. Put in enough money to receive the full employer match, which will help you attain financial independence sooner.

5. For your investment accounts, arrange to have money automatically added to mutual funds, index funds, or ETFs. Choose a specific amount of money to invest on a regular basis. This can help you buy more when prices are low and less when prices are high, making the ups and downs of the market less important.

6. Consider employing tools or software that allow you to save and invest money automatically. Many personal finance apps allow you to set up monthly money transfers, track your progress, and change your savings rate based on your financial goals.

7. Check your automated transfers and investments on a regular basis to ensure they are in line with your financial goals. Change things if necessary, like putting in more money when you earn more or moving your investments around based on how they are doing.

8. Automation helps keep things consistent, but be ready to change your plan if your financial situation changes. If you go through a big life change, such as getting a raise, moving jobs, or incurring large expenses, adjust your automation settings.

Setting up automatic savings and investments simplifies money management. This way, you're less likely to forget to invest money and can build up your fortune over time.

Exercise: Create a Roadmap to Achieving Financial Independence

Creating a clear and effective plan to financial freedom requires several steps. This exercise will assist you in developing an organized plan to accomplish your financial independence goals. Take these steps:

1. Set your financial independence goal.

Explain what being financially independent means to you in simple terms. Is it stopping work early, starting your own business, or being able to follow your interests without worrying about money?

Figure out how much money you need to be financially independent. This is the amount of money that will cover your living costs and help you live the way you want without having to work.

2. Look at your current financial situation.

Check your current financial situation, including what you own, what you owe, how much money you make, and how much you spend.

Determine how much money you have after debts, then review your monthly income and costs. This will help you understand where you are and where you can improve.

3. Determine your objectives and deadlines.

Divide your objective of achieving financial independence into smaller, more manageable tasks. For example, if you want to retire in 15 years, set minor objectives for each year or every few years.

Set deadlines for each objective to keep on track and monitor your progress.

4. Create a plan of action.

Create explicit steps for achieving each goal. This might involve saving more money, paying off debts, or increasing your income through part-time work or progression in your job.

Find the resources you'll need to make your strategy a reality, such as money management software, investment accounts, or financial advisors.

5. Make things mechanized and set them in action.

Set up automatic deposits into your savings and investing accounts based on your plan. To achieve your financial goals, make monthly contributions to your savings account.

Make plans to reduce costs and increase income. Think about how to save money, spend wisely, and create more ways to earn money.

6. Keep an eye on your plan and make changes as needed.

Check how you are doing with each goal often. Keep an eye on how much you own, how much you save, and where you invest to make sure you are doing well.

Change your plan if your financial situation, the market, or your personal goals change. Be open and changeable to keep moving forward towards financial freedom.

What specific financial independence goal is most important to you, and how will achieving it change your lifestyle?
How does your current financial situation compare to your roadmap, and what steps can you take to improve it?
What difficulties may you encounter on your route to financial freedom, and how will you overcome them?

AFTERWORD

Once you complete Mastering Financial Freedom, pause to reflect on the significant transformations you've undergone. By using the ideas and methods in this book, you have prepared yourself with the right way of thinking and tools to gain and keep financial success.

During this journey, you have changed the way you think, created good habits, and put in place practical plans that help you achieve lasting success. You've built a strong base for your financial future by learning how important a positive attitude is and by taking practical steps like investing, budgeting, and making connections.

The exercises and strategies given are not just ideas to think about – they are meant to be used, tried out, and improved as you keep progressing on your journey. The real work starts now as you use these habits in your everyday life and see what happens from your hard work.

Remember, getting to financial freedom takes time and effort. It needs ongoing learning, the ability to adjust, and the strength to bounce back. Face difficulties head-on, enjoy your achievements, and keep working towards your money goals. Your path to being financially free is special, and each step you take gets you closer to the freedom and control you want.

Thank you for letting this book be a part of your money journey. With hard work and determination, you can build the money and freedom you dream about. You have the power to create your future. With a positive attitude and good plans, you are on the right path to making sure you have lasting financial success.

P.S. If this book has helped you and improved your financial journey, I would love to hear your thoughts. Your comments and ideas help a lot and guide others as they make their own changes. Please share how this book has changed your life and inspired you to achieve your goals. Your words can inspire and support people who are trying to find their own path to prosperity. Thank you for joining us and for helping to make the world a happier place. May the light you discovered here continue to shine brightly in all that you create.

www.ingramcontent.com/pod-product-compliance
Lightning Source LLC
Chambersburg PA
CBHW031435210526
45464CB00005B/2217